UNDERSTANDING CRIME
Current Theory and Research

Volume 18
SAGE RESEARCH PROGRESS SERIES IN CRIMINOLOGY

ABOUT THE SERIES

The SAGE RESEARCH PROGRESS SERIES IN CRIMINOLOGY is intended for those professionals and students in the fields of criminology, criminal justice, and law who are interested in the nature of current research in their fields. Each volume in the series—four to six new titles will be published in each calendar year—focuses on a theme of current and enduring concern; and each volume contains a selection of previously unpublished essays . . . drawing on presentations made at the previous year's Annual Meeting of the American Society of Criminology.

Now in its fourth year, the series continues with four new volumes, composed of papers presented at the 31st Annual Meeting of the American Society of Criminology, held in Philadelphia, Pennsylvania, November 7-10, 1979. The volumes in this fourth year of publication include:

- *Taboos in Criminology*
  edited by Edward Sagarin
- *Criminal Justice Research: Models and Findings*
  edited by Barbara R. Price and Phyllis Jo Baunach
- *Improving Management in Criminal Justice*
  edited by Alvin W. Cohn and Benjamin Ward
- *Understanding Crime: Current Theory and Research*
  edited by Travis Hirschi and Michael Gottfredson

Previously published volumes include *Biology and Crime* (C. R. Jeffery, ed.), *Perspectives on Victimology* (William H. Parsonage, ed.), *Police Work: Strategies and Outcomes in Law Enforcement* (David M. Petersen, ed.), *Structure, Law, and Power: Essays in the Sociology of Law* (Paul J. Brantingham and Jack M. Kress, eds.), *Courts and Diversion: Policy and Operations Studies* (Patricia L. Brantingham and Thomas G. Blomberg, eds.), *Violent Crime: Historical and Contemporary Issues* (James A. Inciardi and Anne E. Pottieger, eds.), *Crime, Law and Sanctions: Theoretical Perspectives* (Marvin D. Krohn and Ronald L. Akers, eds.), *The Evolution of Criminal Justice: A Guide for Practical Criminologists* (John P. Conrad, ed.), *Quantitative Studies in Criminology* (Charles Wellford, ed.), *Discretion and Control* (Margaret Evans, ed.), *Theory in Criminology: Contemporary Views* (Robert F. Meier, ed.), *Juvenile Delinquency: Little Brother Grows Up* (Theodore N. Ferdinand, ed.), *Contemporary Corrections: Social Control and Conflict* (C. Ronald Huff, ed.), and *Criminal Justice Planning and Development* (Alvin W. Cohn, ed.).

Comments and suggestions from our readers about this series are welcome.

SERIES EDITORS:

James A. Inciardi
University of Delaware

Ronald L. Akers
University of Iowa

RESEARCH PROGRESS SERIES IN CRIMINOLOGY
VOLUME 18

UNDERSTANDING CRIME

Current Theory and Research

Edited by **Travis Hirschi**
and **Michael Gottfredson**

Published in cooperation with the
AMERICAN SOCIETY of CRIMINOLOGY

SAGE PUBLICATIONS   Beverly Hills   London

For information address:

SAGE Publications, Inc. 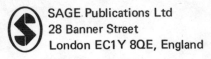 SAGE Publications Ltd
275 South Beverly Drive   28 Banner Street
Beverly Hills, California 90212   London EC1Y 8QE, England

Printed in the United States of America

Library of Congress Cataloging in Publication Data

Main entry under title:

Understanding crime.

    (Sage research progress series in criminology ;
v. 18)
    "Papers presented at the 1979 meetings of the Ameri-
can Society of Criminology in Philadelphia."
    Bibliography: p.
    1. Crime and criminals—Addresses, essays, lectures.
I. Hirschi, Travis.   II. Gottfredson, Michael R.
III. American Society of Criminology.   IV. Series.
HV6028.C736   364.3   80-19376
ISBN 0-8093-1517-9
ISBN 0-8039-1518-7 (pbk.)

FIRST PRINTING

CONTENTS

Travis Hirschi
Michael Gottfredson

State University of
New York, Albany

INTRODUCTION
The Sutherland Tradition in Criminology

The chapters in this volume were selected from the scores of papers presented at the 1979 meetings of the American Society of Criminology in Philadelphia. Two criteria guided our selection: the papers had to be of high quality and they had to be relevant to the influential tradition of criminological thought established by Edwin H. Sutherland.

The second criterion emerged from our initial interest in several papers in what would now be called the social learning tradition, a tradition widely regarded as peculiarly compatible with Sutherland's views. Once these papers had been selected, we decided that thematic balance could be obtained by including papers chosen for the very reason that they were outside, or even contrary to, the Sutherland tradition. This criterion thus excludes little of the work of modern criminology. Sutherland advanced strong views on virtually every theoretical, substantive, and even methodological topic that had been or would be addressed by criminologists. As a result, it is easy to apply his point of view, to note how it has influenced or would have influenced a given piece of research or theorizing.

Sutherland's views on theory and method were themselves heavily influenced by the work of Michael and Adler (1933; see Cressey, 1979). In 1933, Michael, a lawyer, and Adler, a logician, published a critique of criminology entitled *Crime, Law and Social Science*. Their critique brought to criminology the highest standards of logical and empirical adequacy, and criminology failed the test: "There is no scientific knowledge in the field of criminology. . . . Empirical scientific research in criminology cannot be undertaken at the present time" (1933: 390).

Sutherland's initial reaction to the Michael and Adler report was that its condemnation of criminology was "unwarranted": "An attempt is being made to reinstate an extreme rationalism which has already been . . . found to be unproductive. The authors are in effect recommending that we abandon an infant which is showing a health growth and adopt a

7

mummy which has been dead for more than a century" (Geis, 1971, quoting The Sutherland Papers, 1956). Eventually, however, Sutherland came to see the beauty in "extreme rationalism" and the ugliness of raw empiricism. The results of Sutherland's shift to the views of the lawyer and the logician are still with us. The dominant tradition in criminology (Kornhauser, 1978: 189) can thus be traced to rejection of healthy empiricism in favor of a prescientific mode of thought.

The "extreme rationalism" of Michael and Adler gains its appeal from two sources. On the one hand, it makes axiomatic theory the ultimate standard of truth. On the other, it makes empirical research unguided by explicit deductive theory "cheap science or even pseudoscience" (Cressey, 1979: 459). The desire to be scientific (added to the obvious benefits of logical purity) is hard to resist. Once the first step has been taken, and a theory constructed, it is hard to return from the orderly world of true science to the chaos of empirical reality.

Sutherland's first step was to construct the theory of differential association. According to Sutherland (1939), criminal behavior requires socialization into a system of values conducive to the violation of law. Crime cannot be invented by individuals and will not persist in the absence of group support. From the perspective of the group in which the individual is socialized, behavior in conformity with group values is of course not considered "criminal." This label can only be applied by groups with contrary or conflicting values. Because group values are theoretically unrestricted, conflict over the definition of crime is inevitable (see Kornhauser, 1978: 189-204). Notable examples of theorizing within this tradition include Cohen (1955), Miller (1958), Cloward and Ohlin (1960), Wolfgang and Ferracuti (1967), Elliott et al (1979), and Akers et al. (1979), and many modern theories apparently independent of differential association are in fact natural extensions of its views of human nature and of the structure of human society.

There are many ways to explain the influence of Sutherland's theory. Cressey (1979), for example, invokes the analog to Darwin's theory of evolution. In Cressey's view, the theory survives because its broad scope organizes all research and research findings, and provides a solid platform from which to neutralize competitive research and theorizing.

Cressey assumes that differential association is uniquely compatible with the data on criminality, that it adequately explains the known facts about crime, and that its predictions are borne out by original research into fresh areas. Let us begin with the question of prediction. Can delinquency or crime be predicted from individual childhood characteristics? Contrary to an impressive body of research (Glueck and Glueck, 1950; McCord and McCord, 1959; Farrington and West, 1977), differential association says no. Is, say, social disability related to criminality (see Short and Strodt-beck, 1965)? If so, in what direction? Differential association is, for all intents and purposes, silent in the face of such questions. When pushed, the theory is as likely as not to get the answer wrong, to predict the wrong sign for the relation. These assertions about the predictive power of the theory are not really in dispute. As Empey (1978: 328) says, "most criminologists agree" that Sutherland's theory does not meet the test of predictive utility.

A theory with little predictive power may still account for the observed characteristics of a phenomenon (witness the value of natural selection in accounting for the characteristics of living things). How well does differential association account for the observed characteristics of offenders? There are two answers to this question. In one, the theory does very well indeed. When faced with facts about offenders, one merely invokes the phrase "that's differential association" or "that's subculture of violence." Such use of the theory is widely encountered. In fact, Sutherland and Cressey (1978) clearly show that the theory can be used in this way to account for virtually all known correlates of criminality. The other, more stringent test requires *evidence* that differential association or subculture actually provides the link between criminal behavior and the characteristics in question. Such evidence is not provided by the correlations themselves, since these correlations may be used simultaneously as evidence for a competing theory. Nor is it provided by assertions that positive learning of criminal moral codes is a necessary condition for crime (e.g., Elliott et al., 1979), since such assertions are merely restatements of the theory and themselves require empirical support. A recent, thorough review of the relevant research literature concludes that theories in the Sutherland tradition do not meet this more stringent test, that they are, on the contrary, "without foundation in fact" (Hornhauser, 1978: 253).

Since the theory of differential association neither predicts nor explains criminal behavior, its continued dominance cannot be explained on grounds of scientific adequacy. An alternative hypothesis is that differential association and its variants survive for the very reason that they are somehow protected from scientific research and are inimical to the development of healthy theoretical competition.

This brings us to a second, less well known or understood element of the Sutherland tradition, the systematic use of a carefully constructed model of true science in evaluating the contribution of science as ordinarily practiced. Although Sutherland did not invent this strategy, it is misleading to suggest that he first discovered it in Michael and Adler. In fact, in this regard, Michael and Adler were in effect students of Sutherland. Sutherland had for some time before the Michael and Adler report been engaged in the revolt against positivism and quantitative research based on a "multiple factor theory." Prior to Michael and Adler, however, he lacked a consistent strategy for dealing with empirical research. The strategy he eventually adopted is embodied in the theory of differential association which defines the necessary and sufficient causes of crime. Once these causes had been defined, it was possible to treat the correlates of crime as (1) factors consistent with the theory or (2) empirical noise somehow generated by artifacts of the investigator's method of research. This allowed Sutherland to maintain an apparently eclectic, open-minded stance toward the facts while at the same time condemning as non-scientific the multiple factor approach producing them. In other words, Sutherland invented or adopted standards of scientific adequacy that permitted ad hoc interpretation of research findings in ways consistent *only* with the theory of differential association.

Once these standards had been invented, the system was closed to further modification. Subsequent to their invention, research results were certain to be simply further illustration of the power of differential association, competing theories were certain to be based on premises already shown to be faulty in the original construction of differential association, and acceptable theories were certain to be only commentary on or specification of the master theory (Cressey, 1979).

The genius of Sutherland, then, was that as he produced a theory of criminality, he simultaneously produced a science to protect it from research results and from competitive theories. Without its own science, differential association would be just another theory of criminality forced to make its way in a hostile environment. With its own science, differential association could move easily to an environment of friendly research and subservient theorizing, allowing the field to maintain the illusion that it possessed a theory compatible with research and capable of accounting for its results. The fact that differential association was a *sociological* theory also guaranteed the continued domination of a single discipline over the field. Apparently integrated approaches (e.g., subculture of violence) turned out, on inspection, to be largely restatements of the narrow sociological perspective embodied in differential association (Wolfgang and Ferracuti, 1967).

In such a situation, progress or change is likely to come mainly from those outside the sphere of influence of the master perspective. Those unencumbered by this perspective include (1) multiple factor theorists ignorant of the fact that individual qualities and the statistical techniques necessary to study them are irrelevant to crime causation, and (2) theorists ignorant of the principle of normative conflict and thus also ignorant of the fact that the range of human values is unlimited. (The best example is

Kornhauser, 1978). Such theorists could continue to assume that crime may be contrary to the values of the groups in which it occurs, that, in other words, the values defining crime are widely shared. They could therefore further assume that crime may represent not the realization of values but their antithesis or absence.

THE MULTIPLE FACTOR APPROACH

Sutherland's assertion that "no amount of calculation of the risks of different categories of persons will bring us much closer to an understanding of criminal behavior" (1947: 3) is, of course, precisely contrary to the prevailing assumptions of the social and behavioral sciences. Outside criminology, the multiple factor approach has become the dominant perspective of these sciences, accounting for a veritable flood of works on research design and data analysis, as well as the bulk of substantive work. The major statistical problem of the multiple factor approach, that it did not consider the intercorrelations among "factors," has been a major concern in much of this development and had been extensively addressed long before the approach was abandoned by criminologists.

Nonetheless, Sutherland's views have become so firmly rooted in criminology that the death of positivism is taken for granted by a large portion of criminologists. Some even claim that the vestiges of positivism in criminology are evidence that the field is out of touch with developments in twentieth-century philosophy of science (e.g., Matza, 1964; Schur, 1973). Others assert that the positivistic approach is contrary to what is known about the structure of society and the purposes of human action (e.g., Taylor et al., 1973: Ch. 2).

The first four chapters in this volume are within the multiple factor tradition. Although they differ greatly among themselves, each assumes that something useful may be learned about the causes of crime by examining its correlates, that we will indeed be closer to an understanding of criminal behavior when we have calculated "the risks of different categories of persons."

No "factor" traditionally studied by statistical methods has better served the cause of those who would demean the positivistic approach than the "broken home." In some criminological quarters, interest in this factor places the researcher beyond the pale of respectability (Mannheim, 1965: 618). Although textbooks of course continue to cover the history of interest in the broken home in criminological thought, the authors are usually careful to keep their distance from the idea, to place it in the context of a long discredited point of view.

Karen Wilkinson's chapter ("The Broken Home and Delinquent Behavior") clearly shows that children from broken homes are more likely to commit a variety of delinquent acts under a variety of conditions. Her careful research indicates that, for respectable criminologists, interest in the broken home need not be merely historical, and that they need not import the theory of differential association to account for the results.

Another long discredited factor is religion. Sutherland's method of destroying the causal significance of religion is a model of the techniques he used to destroy the multiple factor approach. Consider the following:

> Since crime often involves violation of [the] standard morality, it may *rightfully* be concluded that a *close relationship* exists between crime and the religious institution. . . . And from this it is easy to conclude that "lack of religious training" is the basic cause of crime. However, this conclusion merely emphasizes the fact that some persons do commit crime, and it does not really explain why they do so [Sutherland and Cressey, 1970: 234].

Sutherland's method is simplicity itself. Any correlate of criminality will prove variability in criminal behavior (otherwise correlation is not possible) and nothing else. The explanation of criminality implicit in the correlation therefore finds no support in empirical fact. Explanations without empirical support are of course easily rejected.

The chapter by Rodney Stark, Lori Kent, and Daniel Doyle ("Rediscovering Moral Communities") should go a long way toward restoring the interest of criminologists in the religious factor. It should also warn them against easy acceptance of theories that reject the implications of a correlation before these implications have been examined.

Sutherland did not directly address the environmental design approach to crime causation (the subject of the paper by Taylor, Gottfredson, and Brower, "The Defensibility of Defensible Space") because it was still to come when his text was written. That is not to say, however, that he did not lay the groundwork for coping with factors that had not yet been explicitly addressed: "Almost everything in the universe has been found to be associated in some direct or indirect manner with criminality" (1970: 624).

What else need be said to trivialize the search for the correlates of crime? Any research "discovery" can only add to an already endless litany of alleged causes. Under these conditions, there are two reactions: in one, the criminologist constructs a theory capable of accounting for almost everything in the universe. Such a theory, by definition, will be consistent with any possible correlate of criminality. As a consequence, it will predict nothing and be consistent with everything. In this solution the trivialization of research leads directly to trivialization of theory as well. A second solution to the "everything is correlated" problem is to treat the research literature with the disrespect it so clearly deserves. Both solutions may be applied to defensible space research. For example, if correlates are found, "it is not correct . . . to conclude [that design] is a direct causal factor in crime. Instead, it *can be concluded* that [design] is important to criminality and noncriminality because it determines the kinds of behavior patterns with which persons come in contact" (Sutherland and Cressey, 1978: 226-227; the quote is borrowed from a discussion of marital status of adults, which is said to have "considerable significance in relation to crime").

In other words, Sutherland and Cressey know that no factor has a direct impact on crime and, furthermore, that no intervening mechanism other than differential association can be construed as possibly accounting for the observed association. How they know this, they do not say. Apparently, they are able to infer multivariate relations from a single bivariate association. In any event, had Taylor and his colleagues followed the Sutherland tradition, they would be unlikely to posit such things as "territorial cognitions" as potential mediating variables. For that matter, had they followed the second solution of this tradition, they would be unlikely to be interested in adding yet another correlate to the universe of evidence available to the "behavior patterns" theory. Fortunately, Taylor et al. escaped this tradition.

If the "broken home," religion, and environmental design cause few problems for the theory of differential association, the same cannot be said for family processes. In dealing with these processes, the differential association theorist resembles the student prepared to write an exam about worms who is instead asked to write about elephants: "The elephant has a long trunk. This trunk somewhat resembles a worm. Worms are. . . . (Sutherland and Cressey, 1970: Ch. 10). Fortunately, Gerald Patterson ("Children Who Steal") has been sheltered from definitions favorable to differential association. When he sees an eight year old child emitting "aversive behaviors" at the rate of .73 *per minute*, he does not assume that the child has "associated" wich such behavior patterns inside or outside the home, or that, as of the moment, the child is "neutral" with respect to his or her prospects for future delinquency (cf., Sutherland and Cressey, 1970: 223).

On the contrary, Patterson is willing to entertain the hypothesis that the child is an active participant in his own socialization, that "delinquents" are in fact capable of establishing the behavior patterns to be followed by others:

Antisocial children train their parents. The antisocial behaviors typically have an impact; they are very effective in training adults and peers alike to cease making demands. The child does not have to do chores, nor conform to house rules. Similar techniques are used by the child to train teachers and adults in general to believe that it is not necessary for them to go to school or to achieve a reasonable level if he or she does attend.

Patterson's conclusions are based on close, systematic observation of children interacting with their parents. The field of delinquency of course must decide for itself whether to accept such observations of family processes or to continue to rely on theories that allow observation of these processes without being there.

ALTERNATIVE AND MIXED EXPLANATIONS

If differential association has had a corrosive effect on research, its hegemony over conceptualization has been even more complete. If the competing conceptual scheme originated outside sociology, the fact that crime is socially defined would logically prohibit serious consideration of the scheme, although it may be mentioned in the interest of historical thoroughness. In this tradition, the reader is typically warned in advance of the obvious silliness of the perspective to be described to make clear that the author does not really consider it worthy of consideration.

Our introduction to Robert Burgess's "Family Violence: Implications from Evolutionary Biology" must depart from this tradition. We consider his paper an important, elegant statement of a position too long excluded by illegitimate logic from respectable criminological thought.

Burgess develops the thesis that the ultimate origins and current distribution of child abuse may be found in a single principle of evolutionary biology. Burgess's theory of child abuse applies to all cultures, irrespective of the legal status of the behavior. Burgess may of course be wrong, but the mere existence of his theory denies the logic of the Sutherland tradition: "Although crime and criminality are by definition social phenomena, people have for centuries entertained the notion that they are products of nonsocial causes" (Sutherland and Cressey, 1978: 118). Burgess would not deny that crime is a social phenomenon. He provides a clear definition of the behavior to be explained, which is all that science requires. If child abuse as defined by Burgess were the legal definition of child abuse, Burgess would be advancing a biological explanation of a social behavior that is criminal. Sutherland's logic would lead to the conclusion that the explanation is therefore false. In other words, Sutherland's logic allows the disciplinary referent of variables to determine the truth and falsity of scientific theories.

No aspect of Sutherland's theory of differential association is more provocative than the assertion that murder, rape, robbery, and assault are normative behavior. The most explicit version of this thesis is found in the notion of a "subculture of violence." The putative existence of such a subculture is said to confirm the thesis of differential association (Sutherland and Cressey, 1970: 207).

Wolfgang and Ferracuti have shown that a "subculture of violence" exists in the American urban lower class, and this subculture is carried by families as well as by other groups. (Cf., Kornhauser, 1978: 187.)

One problem with this thesis is that existing evidence appears to point in the other direction. Groups with high rates of violence do not condone or approve of violence. Furthermore, many of their acts of violence are perpetrated on members of their own group. One is then forced through Sutherland's logic to conclude that some groups value their own destruction.[1] Anthony Mawson ("Aggression, Attachment Behavior, and Crimes of Violence") attempts to cut through these facts with the ironic hypothesis that high rate groups have "a relatively strong predisposition for attachment behavior." Such attachment behavior brings them together in social settings under conditions conducive to stress. In these conditions, further attachment seeking results in violence. Pursuit of basic sociability needs thus results in behavior contrary to the values of the group. In an area benumbed by the unsupported assertions of the differential association-subcultural theorists, Mawson's thesis may well stimulate useful thought.

The chapters by Conger ("Juvenile Delinquency") and by Braukmann, Kirigin, and Wolf ("Group Home Treatment Research") are explicitly in the social learning tradition, which may be characterized as a combination of psychological learning principles and differential association. In one branch of social learning theory, operant conditioning from psychology was explicitly paired with Sutherland's theory of differential association, suggesting that Sutherland's along among sociological theories is compatible with learning research. This alliance with Sutherland unfortunately suggested that Sutherland's theoretical opposition was also opposed to established principles of operant conditioning. Put another way, by allying themselves with Sutherland, psychologically oriented theorists have lent their weight to one side of an essentially sociological dispute.

The motto of the revolution against biological positivism that took place early in this century was: *crime is learned.* To those in the vanguard of the revolution, this motto meant only that crime, as such, is not inherited (Sutherland, 1947: 6). Of course, since the revolution (and probably before) no one had believed that crime is inherited (Glueck, 1956). On the contrary, everyone has believed that crime is, in some sense of the term, learned. Given this common assumption, many theorists have felt free to pursue explanations of criminality consistent with the motto of the revolution without endlessly repeating it. Unfortunately, the lack of repetition by some theorists has been mistakenly interpreted as evidence of possible retrogression, of sympathy with prerevolutionary modes of thought.

Sutherland did not make this mistake. On the contrary, he made the motto of the revolution the keystone of his theory of crime. This allowed him to use the theory to suggest that competing theories must have revisionist elements and therefore be unacceptable. By the same token, his theory could not be criticized without the critic casting doubt on his or her own commitment to the revolution.

Enter scholars armed with new-found learning principles in search of a theory of criminality suitable for their exposition. They encounter a theory of crime whose first statement is the motto of the revolution, and the age-old dream of truly interdisciplinary theory is at hand. Precise, interspecific behavioral psychology and sensitive, human symbolic interaction at last reconciled! The combined resources of these great traditions must surely triumph.

Alas, it was too good to be true. As with most intellectual marriages, one partner seeks to dominate. Being basically eclectic and scientific, behavioral psychology is always open to fresh propositions. Being nurtured on rigid conformity to disciplinary principles, symbolic interaction sees any flirtation as a threat to the purity of the sociological approach.

The first points of disagreement came with the restatement of the theory of differential association in operant terms (Burgess and Akers, 1966). When the dust had settled, it turned out that Sutherland's theory was not isomorphic with the motto of the revolution after all, that, indeed, it required substantial modification. When the necessary modifications had been made, Sutherland's theory had lost its distinctive character. It was still possible to say that crime is learned, but it was no longer possible to say that crime is learnd only in the ways specified by Sutherland. In fact, Burgess and Akers were most explicit: "While social learning is, indeed, important and even predominant, it certainly does not exhaust the learning process" (1966: 138).[2]

The current coalition of psychological and sociological approaches to crime, represented by Conger's chapter, has come a long way from the exclusive reliance on the views of Sutherland and Skinner that marked early work. However, it retains the heavy reliance on properties of the environment to the exclusion of properties of the individual that mark the work of both Skinner and Sutherland. (A reliance that helps account for the intitial compatibility of the two approaches.) Sutherland's focus on properties of the environment reflects his rejection of positivism and its focus on individual differences. It also reflects the qualitiative emphasis of symbolic interactionism, which makes the meaningful study of individual differences extremely difficult if not impossible. Skinner's focus on properties of the environment reflects his perhaps heuristic assumption that there are few important differences in individuals, an assumption reinforced by the ease with which behavioral psychology moves from one species to another and by the difficulties involved in studying individual differences under controlled laboratory conditions.

In this connection, Conger's call for the reintroduction of individual differences to the study of crime is most refreshing and highly ironic. There is a body of research and theory for which such a call is unnecessary. This research and theory is easily characterized: it is that portion of criminology rejected in the revolution—i.e., positivistic research based typically on some version of control theory.

In retrospect, it appears that by claiming exclusive possession of the idea that crime is learned, the revolution misrepresented previous work. This work too assumed that crime is learned, but it also assumed that such learning is conditioned by properties of individuals (which properties might be called factors, of which there are many).

Conger's main concern is the continuing (but related) problem of the apparent absence of a motivational component in control theory. Control theorists traditionally assume that the motivation for crime comes from such a variety of sources that no theory can hope to catalog them in any nontrivial way. It is, control theorists assume, sufficient to note that crimes produce pleasures. The real problem is then to identify differences in groups and individuals predictive of pursuit of these pleasures. To a control theorist, the delinquent gang or peer group provides a setting in which individuals are free to pursue the pleasures of crime without fear of negative sanctions. Possessing, as they do, a limited array of such sanctions, peers are relatively ineffective as agents of socialization or of social control. (They may be ineffective for other reasons as well, as Patterson's intriguing discussion of the "adolescent" mother suggests.) If they too enjoy the pleasures of crime, their ability to sanction the criminal behavior of others is largely dissipated, whether they approve or disapprove of it (on the assumption that actions speak louder than words).

Therefore, the persistent finding that peers behave similarly does not necessarily favor social learning theory over other learning theories. One is no more a positive explanation of criminality than the other. To be scientific, the choice among explanations must be based ultimately on empirical evidence, evidence that does not now appear to be available. As Sutherland would *not* have said, the truth of an explanation cannot be judged only by its consistency with a priori principles.

NOTES

1. Control theory too has trouble with this fact, and tends to fall back on opportunity notions to account for the uncomfortable fact that if not each man at least some men, as Oscar Wilde said, kill the thing they love.

2. By Sutherland's own necessary and sufficient criterion, endlessly applied to competing theories and to the multiple factor approach, this fact *falsifies* the theory of differential association (1947: 3). For that matter, the theory of differential association itself contains an assertion that contradicts Sutherland's statement that a theory "consists of a description of the conditions which are always present when a phenomenon occurs and which are never present when the phenomenon does not occur" (1947: 3). Proposition no. 3 in the theory asserts that "the principal part of the learning of criminal behavior occurs within intimate personal groups" (1947: 6). This statistical statement presumably means that not more than 50% of crime is accounted for by other mechanisms. It certainly means that the theory of differential association is not, by Sutherland's own definition, a scientific explanation of crime.

REFERENCES

AKERS, R., M. KROHN, L. LANZA-KADUCE, and M. RADOSEVICH (1979) "Social learning and deviant behavior: a specific test of a general theory." American Sociological Review 44: 636-655.

BURGESS, R., and R. AKERS (1966) "A differential association-reinforcement theory of criminal behavior." Social Problems 14: 128-147.

CLOWARD, R., and L. OHLIN (1960) Delinquency and Opportunity. New York: Free Press.

COHEN, A. (1955) Delinquent Boys. New York: Free Press.

CRESSEY, D. (1979) "Fifty years of criminology." Pacific Sociology Review 22: 457-480.

ELLIOTT, D., S. AGETON, and R. CANTER (1979) "An integrated theoretical perspective on delinquent behavior." Journal of Research in Crime and Delinquency 16: 3-27.

EMPEY, L. T. (1978) American Delinquency. Homewood, IL: Dorsey.

GEIS, G. (1971) "Introduction to the reprint edition." J. Michael and M. Adler (eds.) Crime, Law and Social Science. Montclair: Patterson-Smith.

GLUECK, S. and E. T. GLUECK (1950) Unraveling Juvenile Delinquency. Cambridge, MA: Harvard Univ. Press.

GLUECK, S. (1956, 1964) "Theory and fact in criminology." British Journal of Delinquency 7: 92-109. Also printed in Ventures in Criminology. Cambridge, MA: Harvard Univ. Press.

KORNHAUSER, R. (1978) Social Sources of Delinquency: An Appraisal of Analytic Models. Chicago: Univ. of Chicago Press.

MANNHEIM, H. (1965) Comparative Criminology. Boston: Houghton Mifflin.

MATZA, D. (1964) Delinquency and Drift. New York: John Wiley.

McCORD, W. and J. McCORD (1959) Origins of Crime. New York: Columbia Univ. Press.

MICHAEL, J. and M. ADLER (1933, 1971) Crime, Law and Social Science. Montclair: Patterson-Smith.

MILLER, W. B. (1958) "Lower class culture as a generating milieu of gang delinquency." Journal of Social Issues 14: 5-19.

SCHUR, E. M. (1973) Radical Non-Interaction. Englewood Cliffs, NJ: Prentice-Hall.

SHORT, J. and F. STRODTBECK (1965) Group Process and Gang Delinquency. Chicago: Univ. of Chicago Press.

SUTHERLAND, E. (1947) Principles of Criminology. Philadelphia: Lippincott.

SUTHERLAND, E. and D. CRESSEY (1970, 1978) Criminology. Philadelphia: Lippincott.

TAYLOR, I., P. WALTON, and J. YOUNG (1973) The New Criminology: For a Social Theory of Deviance. London: Routledge & Kegan Paul.

WEST, D. J. and D. P. FARRINGTON (1977) The Delinquent Way of Life. New York: Crane Russak.

WOLFGANG, M. and F. FERRACUTI (1967) The Subculture of Violence. London: Tavistock.

Karen Wilkinson
Memphis State University

THE BROKEN HOME AND DELINQUENT BEHAVIOR:
An Alternative Interpretation
of Contradictory Findings

Speculation and research regarding the broken home as a cause of delinquent behavior has existed since the early years of delinquency research (Monahan, 1957a; Wilkinson, 1974). It has been assumed that the loss of a parent, usually the father and especially if through divorce, causes the child to be unhappy and/or disrupts parental control, which results in delinquent behavior. Though this appears to be a sensible assumption, broken home research has not provided consistent support for either the underlying assumptions or the broken home-delinquent behavior relationship itself.

This lack of consistent support could lead to the conclusion that the broken home must not be a significant cause of delinquent behavior and therefore should be ignored. However, we propose that ignoring the broken home would be a mistake for two reasons. First, the lack of consistent findings may be partly because different studies have operationalized critical variables (i.e., "broken home," "delinquent behavior") in different ways and have utilized samples of dissimilar composition. The broken home may be associated with delinquent behavior under some conditions and according to some definitions but not others. These variations need to be specified and interpreted.

The second reason is that an increasing proportion of children are living in homes broken by divorce. Between 1960 and 1978, the proportion of two-parent families among all families with children under the age of 18 declined from 91.5% to 81.1% (U.S. Bureau of the Census, 1979). These

AUTHOR'S NOTE: This chapter is based on data gathered as part of a larger study of "Community Tolerance and Measures of Delinquency" supported by a grant from the National Institute of Mental Health (MH 22350), Maynard L. Erickson, principal investigator. The author wishes to express her gratitude to the entire research staff (especially B. Grant Stitt, James Creechan, and Gary Jensen) for their work in gathering the data and preparing it for analysis.

proportions include reconstituted families (those with step-parents) as well as families with both natural parents, so the proportion of children living with both natural parents is actually lower. It has been estimated that if the current trend continues, about 45% of the children born in 1977 will live in a one-parent family for at least several months before the age of 18 (Glick and Norton, 1977). If more children will be living in broken homes, knowledge of the relation between the broken home and delinquent behavior will be of greater practical significance.

The purpose of this investigation is to examine the relation between the broken home and delinquent behavior under a variety of conditions. The goal is to determine if the strength of the relation is affected by these conditions. This is accomplished both by reviewing the evidence of previously published studies and by presenting new evidence.

REVIEW OF THE LITERATURE

Two methods have characterized research on the broken home: (1) research on the prevalence of the broken home among adjudicated (or otherwise officially categorized) delinquents compared with its prevalence in the general population, and (2) research on the association between the stability of the home and self-reported delinquent behavior, almost all of which was not officially recognized. All of the early research used official measures of delinquency. This method of assessing the *etiological* importance of the broken home was once regarded as adequate. The development of the self-report method has made these findings less convincing, but studies of this type are still conducted (e.g., Datesman and Scarpitti, 1975; Offord et al., 1979).

Although we are interested primarily in the results of studies using the self-report method, the results of the studies utilizing official data deserve to be mentioned. Nearly all of the official data studies provide evidence that children from broken homes are overrepresented in juvenile courts and juvenile institutions (e.g., Monahan, 1957a, 1957b; Chilton and Markle, 1972; Rosen, 1969). Although some have concluded from such findings that broken homes cause delinquent behavior (Toby, 1957; Barker and Adams, 1961), others prefer the conclusion that children from broken homes are likely to be selected for court attention because of their perceived need for help and not necessarily because they are more delinquent than children from intact homes (Nye, 1958). Indeed, Thomas and Sieverdes (1975) show that family instability is an influential factor in the decision-making process at intake.

Studies utilizing self-reported delinquent behavior avoid the selective bias problem of studies using official records. Unlike the official delinquency studies, the self-reported delinquency studies have not shown children from broken homes to be significantly more delinquent than those from intact homes. Nye (1958), Dentler and Monroe (1961), and Hirschi (1969) have all reported that there is a relation between the broken home and delinquent behavior, but that it is a weak one. Gold (1970: 127), however, maintains that "the factor of broken homes relates reliably, meaningfully, and interestingly to measures of delinquent behavior."

Surprisingly little investigation beyond the simple relation between the broken home and delinquent behavior has been conducted. There are some indications, however, that (1) the broken home is more strongly related to the commission of some offenses than to others and, (2) sex, race and/or socioeconomic status may influence the strength of the relationship.[1]

Regarding the type of offense, Austin's (1978) and Dentler and Monroe's (1961) findings are consistent in that both found the broken home to be unrelated to theft. Hirschi's (1969) finding of a weak association between the broken home and delinquency may be partly because of the predominance of theft items in his delinquency index (four of the six offenses are taken from Dentler and Monroe's theft scale). Austin (1978), however, did find father absence to be related to white boys' and white girls' auto theft. In addition, father absence is associated with white girls' vandalism and assault (Austin, 1978). Broken homes seem to be more strongly related to "ungovernable" types of behavior (e.g., truancy, running away, premarital sex) than to other types of delinquent conduct (Nye, 1958). Also, broken homes were found to be more related to marijuana use than to alcohol use, theft, or vandalism, though this association is slight (Hennessey et al., 1978).

In addition to variations in the association by type of offense, the association also seems to be stronger for some types of children than for others. First, girls may be more affected by family instability than boys (Nye, 1958; Gold, 1970; Austin, 1978). Second, the child's race may be important but there is only evidence (from self-reports) that this is true of girls. In Hirschi's data (1969), black and white boys' delinquent behavior was found to be similarly affected by the absence of their fathers. Using the same data source, Austin (1978) found the relation between father-absence and delinquency to be stronger for white girls than for black girls. Third, socioeconomic status may be relevant, but existing evidence is inconclusive. While Austin (1978) argues that the broken home is associated with delinquency even among more affluent white girls, Hennessey et al. (1978) maintain that broken homes have no effect on delinquent behavior in their sample of middle-class juveniles.

The evidence provided here will add to existing knowledge of the broken home-delinquent behavior relationship in several ways. First, data on the nature of the offenses associated with the stability of the home will be examined. Second, evidence is provided regarding sex differences in the strength of the relationship. Finally, the scope of knowledge of the conditions under which the broken home is influential will be broadened by examining the relationship separately for Mexican-Americans and Anglo-Americans, Protestants and Catholics, and urban and rural residents.

RESEARCH DESIGN

The data for this study were drawn from a survey conducted in six southern Arizona high schools during the fall of 1975. Three of the high schools (two public, one Catholic) are located in an urban community with a population of about 400,000. Its economy is based on a mixture of mining, manufacturing, tourism, a military base, and a university. The other three schools (all public schools) are in smaller communities with populations varying from about 1,200 to 8,000. These communities can be characterized as a mining town, a tourist town, and a ranching town. From all schools combined, 3,267 questionnaires were collected.

In all schools, participation in the surveys was voluntary, but the schools differed slightly in the conditions required by school officials for administering the questionnaires. All but one school allowed the questionnaires to be administered in regular classes throughout the school day. In this school, one period was set aside for all student volunteers to leave their classes to participate in the survey. In all cases, the students were assured that their participation was strictly voluntary and that their answers were anonymous and confidential.

Assurance of anonymity was particularly important to obtain valid self-reports of delinquent behavior. The self-report method is used here rather than official records of delinquency because findings from official records would be incomplete and ambiguous. Official records include only a small proportion of all young offenders. This is a critical disadvantage because those juveniles who appear on record are not representative of the total population of law-violating juveniles. Since it is likely that the official definition of "the delinquent" is affected by many factors other than the behavior itself (including the stability of the home), the self-report method is better in that "the delinquent" is defined only by the reported behavior. In other words, self-reported data are not biased by the official reactors' beliefs about who is in need of help or control. While we do not maintain that self-reported delinquency is perfectly representative of the "true" amount and nature of delinquent behavior, we do consider it to be a better estimate of the true rate than official records.

Proceeding from this assumption, students were asked to report how many times in the previous twelve months they had committed each of twenty delinquent and status offenses. From the twenty offenses, these eight were selected to examine their relation to the broken home: vandalism, assault, shoplifting, auto theft, marijuana use, drinking alcohol, truancy, and running away.[2] These offenses were chosen partly because they represent the broad range of juvenile misbehavior and also because they enable some comparison of these findings with those of previous studies.

The broken home has been defined in past research in a variety of ways. Some researchers have broadly defined the broken home as one in which one or both natural parents are absent (e.g., Hennessey et al., 1978; Gold, 1970). Others have restricted the definition to homes without natural fathers (e.g., Hirschi, 1969; Austin, 1978). The latter, slightly more restrictive definition is used here for two reasons. First, father-absence is more frequent than mother-absence. While it is somewhat more likely now than in the past for fathers to gain custody of their children after a divorce, in 1976 about 1% of children lived with their fathers only while 16% lived with their mothers only (Glick and Norton, 1977). Therefore, findings regarding the effects of mother-absence would have limited generalizability. The second reason for limiting the definition to father-absence is the recognition that the absence of a mother or the absence of both parents may have different effects than the absence of a father. This possibility has only rarely been investigated but there are some indications that different types of parental absence should be analyzed separately (Wilkinson, 1978).[3]

Two questions were used to determine whether a child was from an intact home or a broken home. One asked who was acting as the child's father; the other asked who was acting as the child's mother. Respondents who reported that both natural parents were living at home were classified as living in intact homes (2,261 respondents or 69.7%). Those who reported living with their natural mothers and any other "fathers" besides their natural ones or with no fathers at all were classified as living in father-absent homes (648 respondents or 20.0%). Respondents who reported living with their natural fathers but not their natural mothers or who had neither natural parent living at home were excluded. Their exclusion reduces the number of cases by 270 (or 8.3%), leaving 2,909 usable cases.

Only a few words of explanation are needed for the other variables used in this study. Sex, ethnicity, and religious affiliation were determined by directly asking respondents to categorize themselves as male or female and identifying their own ethnic status and their own religious affiliation. Students who attended the three high schools surveyed in the metropolitan area were considered to be urban residents, while those who attended high schools in the small towns were considered to be rural residents.

FINDINGS

In this sample of southern Arizona students, proportionately more boys and girls from father-absent homes report each of the offenses than do boys and girls from intact homes (Table 1.1). The consistency in the direction of the relationship across all offenses is important even though the associations are sometimes small. The strength of the associations (and the presumed effect of father-absence) is not the same, however, for all types of children. Before examining these differences, variations in the relationship by offense and the degree of consistency of these findings with prior research are considered.

The Nature of the Offenses, Gender, and Father-Absence

Several studies have shown father-absence and theft to be unrelated. The negligible association between father absence and boys' shoplifting is consistent with these studies, while the stronger association for girls' shoplifting is not (Table 1.1). For both boys and girls, the association between father-absence and auto theft is lower than that identified in Austin's (1978) study. In general, though, it must be concluded that father-absence has only a slight association with these two types of theft, but the effect is stronger for girls than for boys.

Previous research in California (Austin, 1978) identified moderate associations between father-absence and white girls' vandalism (gamma = .37) and assault (gamma = .33) but very weak ones for white and black boys (gammas were .11 or less). The findings reported in Table 1.1 disagree because there is only a negligible association between father-absence and girls' vandalism, a low association between father-absence and girls' assault, and a low association (but still a stronger one than in the California data) between father-absence and boys' vandalism. The two studies agree, however, in finding essentially no association between father-absence and boys' assault.

In this sample, the boys' drinking of alcohol is associated with father-absence in about the same strength as is marijuana use (gammas are .17 and .19). The same pattern exists for girls (gammas are .20 and .23). These similarities are inconsistent with the finding among midwestern middle-

TABLE 1.1 Father-Absence and Delinquent Behavior by Gender

	Boys			Girls		
	Percentage[a] and Number Reporting Offense from:			Percentage[a] and Number Reporting Offense from:		
	Intact Homes	Father-Absent Homes	Gamma	Intact Homes	Father-Absent Homes	Gamma
Vandalism	33.1 (370)	44.1 (131)	.23**	11.2 (123)	13.1 (44)	.09
Assault	24.2 (270)	27.0 (79)	.07	8.6 (95)	12.4 (42)	.20*
Shoplifting	43.1 (482)	45.3 (135)	.05	28.6 (315)	38.4 (129)	.22**
Auto theft	13.5 (152)	16.7 (49)	.12	6.9 (76)	9.5 (32)	.17
Marijuana use	42.4 (476)	51.0 (151)	.17**	40.1 (439)	50.0 (169)	.20**
Drinking	74.4 (836)	81.0 (239)	.19*	69.0 (762)	77.9 (265)	.23**
Truancy	53.0 (599)	65.8 (196)	.26**	47.7 (527)	66.7 (226)	.37**
Running away	9.1 (102)	15.7 (46)	.30**	10.1 (112)	16.4 (56)	.27**

*p < .05 > .01
**p < .01

[a]For this and subsequent tables, the proportions are those who reported committing the offense one or more times in the previous 12 months. The responses for each offense were dichotomized: 0 = no instances of the offense reported; 1 = 1 or more instances of the offense reported.

class adolescents that father-absence is more relevant to marijuana use than it is to drinking alcohol (Hennessey et al., 1978).

Although there are these inconsistencies, there are two findings consistent with prior research. These data support Nye's (1958) finding that father-absence has more impact on "ungovernable" conduct (truancy and running away) than on criminal conduct. This is true of both boys and girls. Another common contention, that girls' behavior is more adversely affected by the broken home than is boys', receives limited support. Father-absence has more of an "effect" on boys than on girls for only one offense (vandalism), while father-absence and three offenses (assault, shoplifting, and truancy) are more closely associated for girls than for boys.

For the remaining offenses, however, there is little difference in the strength of the associations for boys and girls. Even though father-absence may have more to do with causing female delinquency than male delinquency, it is only *slightly* more important for girls and the degree of differential importance differs by offense.

So far we have identified a number of differences between the findings from this sample of southern Arizona youth and those of prior studies. One of the possible explanations for this is that all but one of the previously cited self-report studies (the study of middle-class youth, Hennessey et al., 1978) utilized data collected prior to 1966. Thus, the differences identified may be because of change in the effect of father-absence over time. On the other hand, the time interval may be irrelevant, and the differences may be explained by variations in the characteristics of the samples (such as geographic location, socioeconomic status, ethnicity, and religion). If the effect of father-absence differs according to these characteristics, comparing findings from different samples can only be done by controlling for these characteristics. An investigation of this possibility is undertaken here by examining the relation between father-absence and delinquent behavior controlling for ethnicity, religion, and residence. After the findings for all three variables are presented, a frame of reference for understanding the associations will be discussed.

Ethnicity

This examination of ethnicity, the broken home, and delinquent behavior is unique in that Anglo-Americans are compared with Mexican-Americans or Chicanos.[4] When ethnicity has been the subject of broken home research, blacks have been compared with whites (e.g., Austin, 1978; Datesman and Scarpitti, 1975; Willie, 1967). In this study, however, the largest minority group is the Mexican-American group, comprising 21% of the sample.

Father-absence and delinquent behavior are positively associated for both Anglo youth and Mexican-American youth (Tables 1.2 and 1.3). There are some differences in the strength of the association, but the differences are primarily among girls. For boys, the relations between father-absence and six of the offenses are essentially the same regardless of ethnicity (Table 1.2). But for truancy and running away, father-absence is more important for Anglo boys than for Chicano boys. Actually, father-absence has very little to do with Chicano boys' reports of these behaviors and has more relevance for their reports of vandalism, marijuana use, and drinking.

TABLE 1.2 Father-Absence and Male Delinquent Behavior by Ethnicity

| | Anglo-American | | | Mexican-American | | |
| | Percentage and Number Reporting Offense from: | | | Percentage and Number Reporting Offense from: | | |
	Intact Homes	Father-Absent Homes	Gamma	Intact Homes	Father-Absent Homes	Gamma
Vandalism	32.4 (246)	44.4 (95)	.25**	34.3 (87)	46.6 (27)	.25
Assault	22.7 (171)	27.2 (58)	.12	26.3 (67)	27.3 (15)	.03
Shoplifting	39.7 (301)	43.3 (93)	.07	51.0 (129)	55.2 (32)	.08
Auto theft	12.0 (91)	14.1 (30)	.09	16.3 (42)	19.6 (11)	.11
Marijuana use	41.8 (318)	51.6 (111)	.20**	44.8 (115)	56.1 (32)	.22
Drinking	72.7 (553)	79.7 (173)	.19*	78.5 (201)	85.5 (47)	.23
Truancy	53.0 (405)	66.8 (145)	.28**	53.1 (137)	59.7 (34)	.13
Running away	7.8 (59)	15.0 (32)	.35**	10.9 (28)	12.7 (7)	.09

*$p < .05 > .01$
**$p < .01$

For girls, in contrast, truancy and drinking alcohol are the only offenses where father-absence is similarly associated for Anglo-Americans and Chicanos (Table 1.3). Assault and marijuana use are both more closely associated with father-absence for Anglo girls than for Mexican-American girls. These differences are overshadowed, however, by the findings for the remaining four offenses (vandalism, shoplifting, auto theft, running away) which show that father-absence matters more to Mexican-American girls than to Anglo girls.

Religion

In this sample, there are more Catholics than Protestants: 48% declared themselves to be Catholic, 31% Protestant, and 21% Mormon, Jewish,

TABLE 1.3 Father-Absence and Female Delinquent Behavior by Ethnicity

| | Anglo-American | | | Mexican-American | | |
| | Percentage and Number Reporting Offense from: | | | Percentage and Number Reporting Offense from: | | |
	Intact Homes	Father-Absent Homes	Gamma	Intact Homes	Father-Absent Homes	Gamma
Vandalism	10.7 (86)	12.5 (31)	.09	10.5 (22)	15.0 (9)	.20
Assault	8.2 (66)	12.0 (30)	.21	10.4 (22)	11.7 (7)	.06
Shoplifting	27.6 (222)	35.7 (89)	.19*	32.9 (69)	51.7 (31)	.37**
Auto theft	7.2 (58)	8.4 (21)	.09	5.2 (11)	16.4 (10)	.57**
Marijuana use	39.0 (313)	51.6 (129)	.25**	45.2 (95)	48.4 (30)	.06
Drinking	69.2 (560)	79.3 (199)	.26**	69.2 (146)	79.4 (50)	.26
Truancy	48.5 (391)	67.1 (167)	.37**	43.2 (92)	64.5 (40)	.41**
Running away	10.4 (84)	13.9 (35)	.17	8.5 (18)	22.6 (14)	.52**

**p < .05 > .01
**p < .01

other religion, or nonaffiliated. One reason for the high proportion of Catholic respondents is the inclusion of a Catholic high school in the sample. Even without this school, however, there would be about equal numbers of Catholics and Protestants.

The relation between father-absence and delinquent behavior differs for Catholics and Protestants, but it is not consistently stronger for one group rather than the other. There are differences by offense and gender. For boys, the difference in religion is most important for drinking alcohol and using marijuana (Table 1.4). In both cases, Catholic boys' behavior is associated with father-absence while father-absence has little to do with Protestant boys' behavior. On the other hand, the association between father-absence and vandalism and truancy is somewhat stronger for Pro-

TABLE 1.4   Father-Absence and Male Delinquent Behavior by Religion

| | Catholic | | | Protestant | | |
| | Percentage and Number Reporting Offense from: | | | Percentage and Number Reporting Offense from: | | |
	Intact Homes	Father-Absent Homes	Gamma	Intact Homes	Father-Absent Homes	Gamma
Vandalism	36.6 (201)	46.9 (60)	.21*	28.4 (95)	43.8 (39)	.33**
Assault	25.3 (139)	27.4 (34)	.05	21.0 (70)	25.8 (23)	.14
Shoplifting	46.5 (255)	50.0 (64)	.07	38.6 (130)	42.7 (38)	.09
Auto theft	13.7 (76)	18.4 (23)	.17	14.2 (48)	18.0 (16)	.14
Marijuana use	43.2 (239)	55.9 (71)	.25**	41.8 (141)	46.2 (42)	.09
Drinking	79.4 (440)	90.3 (112)	.41**	69.8 (236)	74.7 (68)	.12
Truancy	48.7 (271)	59.8 (76)	.22*	54.9 (186)	70.3 (64)	.32**
Running away	9.2 (51)	16.9 (21)	.34*	7.4 (25)	12.4 (11)	.28

*p < .05 > .01
**p < .01

testant boys than Catholic boys. Finally, controlling for religion has essentially no effect on changing the small associations originally found for boys' assault, shoplifting, and auto theft.

Religious affiliation has quite a startling effect on the relation between father-absence and girls "ungovernable" behavior (Table 1.5). For truancy, the original moderate relation is maintained for both Catholic and Protestant girls, but the running away relationship is not. We discover that father-absence and running away are hardly related among Protestant girls, but moderately related for Catholic girls. Another important difference is in the relation between father-absence and auto theft. For Catholic girls, it is a positive relationship of moderate strength while for Protestant girls it is a negligible, *negative* relationship. Catholic girls from father-absent

TABLE 1.5   Father-Absence and Female Delinquent Behavior by Religion

| | Catholic | | | Protestant | | |
| | Percentage and Number Reporting Offense from: | | | Percentage and Number Reporting Offense from: | | |
	Intact Homes	Father-Absent Homes	Gamma	Intact Homes	Father-Absent Homes	Gamma
Vandalism	11.5 (64)	14.6 (21)	.14	8.9 (31)	9.8 (11)	.05
Assault	8.6 (48)	13.9 (20)	.26	6.9 (24)	7.0 (8)	.01
Shoplifting	31.4 (175)	40.3 (58)	.19*	21.8 (76)	35.4 (40)	.32**
Auto theft	5.7 (32)	11.7 (17)	.37*	7.1 (25)	6.2 (7)	−.08
Marijuana use	43.8 (243)	51.0 (74)	.14	35.8 (124)	50.4 (57)	.29**
Drinking	72.1 (405)	79.5 (116)	.20	65.8 (229)	78.8 (89)	.32**
Truancy	42.5 (238)	64.4 (94)	.42**	51.0 (178)	70.4 (81)	.39**
Running away	8.8 (49)	17.1 (25)	.37**	12.6 (44)	15.7 (18)	.13

*p < .05 > .01
**p < .01

homes also appear more likely to commit assault, while the type of home has no effect on Protestant girls' commission of assault. Father-absence and three of the offenses are somewhat more strongly related for Protestant girls than for Catholic girls: there are moderate relationships for shoplifting, drinking alcohol, and using marijuana for Protestants but low ones for Catholics.

Residence

The three rural schools produced one-third of the respondents in this survey. Unlike the findings for ethnicity and religion, there is a fairly high degree of consistency in the findings for residence: The relation between father-absence and most offenses is stronger for rural residents than for urban residents. Once again, this effect is stronger for girls than for boys. Father-absence and delinquent behavior are more closely associated for rural boys than urban boys for four offenses (vandalism, shoplifting, auto theft, and drinking) (Table 1.6), while the associations are stronger for rural girls for all offenses except marijuana use (Table 1.7). Residence has little to do with either the association between father-absence and boys' assault, marijuana use, truancy, and running away or with the association between father-absence and girls' marijuana use.

INTERPRETIVE DISCUSSION

This summary of the findings demonstrates that the relation between father-absence and delinquent behavior is not a simple one. Under some conditions and for some offenses, father-absence appears to be very important in understanding delinquent behavior, while under other conditions it is not. Rather than further clouding understanding of the role of father-absence in causing delinquent behavior, these disparate findings may actually help to illuminate it. It is possible that father-absence is not consistently associated with delinquent behavior because it has different meanings for children living in different social contexts. More specifically, the broken home's impact on delinquent behavior appears to be greatest in social contexts characterized by relatively low tolerance of divorce and lowest in more divorce-tolerant social contexts.

The findings by residence (showing that father-absence matters less in urban boys' and girls' delinquency than to that of rural boys and girls) provide support for this interpretation. It is commonly assumed that disapproval of divorce is more characteristic of rural than of urban communities (Levinger, 1965). Even without conclusive evidence that this is true, it is logical to assume greater divorce tolerance in urban areas because divorce rates are higher in urban areas than in rural ones (U.S. Bureau of the Census, 1978) and because urban residents are likely to be less conservative and more open to change than are rural residents. Since divorce constitutes change, urban residents would be more accepting of it.

If there is more disapproval of divorce in rural communities, the problems of rural divorced families are compounded by their acceptance of the community norm that their divorce is a shameful act. Furthermore, the children of such families may experience more community stigma or rejection than their urban counterparts both because of the difference in divorce disapproval and because rural community structure permits the

TABLE 1.6 Father-Absence and Male Delinquent Behavior by Residence

| | Urban | | | Rural | | |
| | Percentage and Number Reporting Offense from: | | | Percentage and Number Reporting Offense from: | | |
	Intact Homes	Father-Absent Homes	Gamma	Intact Homes	Father-Absent Homes	Gamma
Vandalism	35.1 (263)	43.3 (91)	.17*	29.0 (107)	46.0 (40)	.35**
Assault	23.4 (174)	25.8 (54)	.07	25.8 (96)	29.8 (25)	.10
Shoplifting	40.4 (303)	40.5 (85)	.00	48.5 (179)	56.8 (50)	.17
Auto Theft	13.5 (102)	14.8 (31)	.05	13.5 (50)	21.4 (18)	.27
Marijuana use	43.5 (327)	51.2 (108)	.15	40.1 (149)	50.6 (43)	.21
Drinking	73.9 (555)	79.5 (167)	.16	75.3 (281)	84.7 (72)	.29
Truancy	53.6 (405)	65.4 (138)	.24**	51.9 (194)	66.7 (58)	.30*
Running away	7.7 (58)	13.8 (29)	.32**	11.9 (44)	20.2 (17)	.31

*p < .05 > .01
**p < .01

disapproval to be more consequential in day-to-day life. If rural life is less anonymous than urban life, the rural family's divorce and circumstances leading up to it are more likely to be known throughout the community, and children are more likely to be recognized as representatives of particular families. Thus, a much higher proportion of the rural child's daily contacts would be with people who know of his parents' divorce than would be true of the urban child's. The rural child's belief that his parents' divorce is wrong may be enhanced if he or she receives differential treatment from others. The child may then develop less respect for his or her parent(s), and parental attachment would weaken.

TABLE 1.7   Father-Absence and Female Delinquent Behavior by Residence

| | Urban | | | Rural | | |
| | Percentage and Number Reporting Offense from: | | | Percentage and Number Reporting Offense from: | | |
	Intact Homes	Father-Absent Homes	Gamma	Intact Homes	Father-Absent Homes	Gamma
Vandalism	11.7 (86)	11.8 (27)	.01	10.2 (37)	15.7 (17)	.24
Assault	7.5 (55)	10.0 (23)	.16	11.0 (40)	17.6 (19)	.27
Shoplifting	27.5 (203)	30.0 (68)	.06	30.9 (112)	56.0 (61)	.48**
Auto theft	8.0 (59)	8.3 (19)	.02	4.6 (17)	11.8 (13)	.47**
Marijuana use	41.7 (306)	50.7 (116)	.18*	36.7 (133)	48.6 (53)	.24*
Drinking	69.8 (518)	75.7 (174)	.15	67.4 (244)	82.7 (91)	.40**
Truancy	48.9 (361)	66.1 (150)	.34**	45.2 (166)	67.9 (76)	.44**
Running away	8.6 (64)	13.1 (30)	.23	13.2 (48)	23.2 (26)	.33*

*p < .05 > .01
**p < .01

According to control theory, weak parental attachment is a significant reason for delinquent behavior. Children who do not care about their parent(s) are not likely to worry about their reaction to their behavior and are therefore free to deviate (Hirschi, 1969: 88). The weakening of parental attachment would not be as likely to happen to urban children of divorce because they would be less likely to regard their parents' divorce as deviant or shameful.

The degree of divorce tolerance may also explain why girls are more affected by father-absence than boys. More emphasis is placed on the importance of marriage and family in female role socialization than in male role socialization because of the expectation that a girl's major adult roles will be "wife" and "mother" while a boy's major role will be "breadwinner." If girls learn to revere family stability more than boys do, their disapproval of divorce would be greater than boys' and the weakening of parental attachment following their parents' divorce may be more significant. The argument that such socialization differences are now only slight is not inconsistent with the findings presented here because they do not indicate girls to be greatly more affected by father-absence than boys. It is possible, though, that earlier studies found greater sex differences because there were greater differences in the attitudes of boys and girls regarding family stability.[5]

Therefore, there should be greater sex differences in the influence of the broken home in cultures or subcultures where boys and girls are socialized more traditionally. Sex role differences tend to be more pronounced in Mexican-American families than in Anglo families (Murrillo, 1971; Mirande, 1977). Even though they may not be as rigid as they once were (Stoddard, 1973), they may cause Mexican-American boys and girls to have much different levels of divorce tolerance. The divorce tolerance of Anglo boys and girls may be more similar. In support of this interpretation, the relation between father-absence and Mexican-American girls' delinquency is moderate to substantial for four offenses (Table 1.3) while the relationship for Mexican-American boys over all offenses is only low at best (Table 1.2). The differences between Anglo boys (Table 1.2) and Anglo girls (Table 1.3) are not as great.

A similar pattern exists in the findings by residence. The relation between father-absence and five of the offenses (assault, shop-lifting, auto theft, drinking, and truancy) is much stronger for rural girls than for rural boys (Tables 1.6 and 1.7). In contrast, urban boys and girls appear to be quite similar in the effect of the broken home on their behavior (Tables 1.6 and 1.7). Here again, more traditional sex role socialization practices (assumed to be characteristic of rural areas) may be responsible for making divorce a more significant event for girls than for boys.

Although the above findings fit the "divorce tolerance" framework, some of the findings appear to constitute negative evidence. One of the potentially problematic findings is that Chicano boys' ungovernable behavior is less affected by the absence of the father than is the Anglo boys' behavior (Table 1.2). This is inconsistent with the framework if it is true that familism is a more significant ideal for Chicanos than for Anglos. While the influence of this ideal on Chicano behavior has been debated, it is commonly maintained that the family is the most important institution in Mexican-American society and that an individual's family role is his/her most important role (Murrillo, 1971; Mirande, 1977). Research by Grebler et al. (1970) on such features of Mexican-American family life as living arrangements, visiting patterns, and dependence on kin questions the reality of the familism ideal. At the same time, however, their research also shows that most Mexican-Americans believe that Mexican-American family ties are stronger than those of most Americans. Furthermore, there is evidence that marital instability in the southwestern United States is lower for Mexican-Americans than for either Anglos or blacks (Eberstein and Frisbie, 1976).

If the family is more important to Chicanos than to Anglos, Chicanos should also be less tolerant of divorce than Anglos, and their delinquent behavior should show more of an effect of father-absence. Instead, father-absence and most offenses are similarly associated for Anglo boys and Chicano boys. For running away and truancy, Anglos are *more* influenced by father-absence than Chicanos. It is possible that instead of weakening parental attachment, the separation of the Chicano boy's parents may in some ways actually strengthen his attachment to the family. Traditionally, Mexican-American sons have been expected to assume paternal authority in the father's absence (Rubel, 1970). If this custom is observed, father-absence would encourage more adultlike behavior among Chicanos (especially among eldest sons) and mitigate the impact of divorce intolerance.

This explanation is more convincing when we recall that Chicano girls are generally more influenced by father-absence than Anglo girls (Table 1.3). Because of the familism ideal, Chicanos would view their parents' separation as more of a deviation than would Anglo-American girls. Unlike their brothers, however, Mexican-American girls would not acquire responsibility for the family when the father leaves. The difference between Anglo-American girls and Mexican-American girls in their idealization of the family would remain as an explanation for the differences in the association between father-absence and delinquency.

The second apparently problematic finding is that the relation between father-absence and delinquent behavior is not consistently stronger for Catholics than for Protestants. Because of differences in church doctrine, Catholics would be expected to be less tolerant of divorce than Protestants. In Catholicism, marriage is a sacrament, and great emphasis is placed on the indissolubility of it. Furthermore, people who remarry are considered to be "in serious sin" (Cassidy, 1972). Children who believe their parents to be immoral would seem to be particularly likely to be less attached to them.

Before conceding that this finding contradicts the "divorce tolerance" framework, it would be necessary to ascertain whether or not Catholics actually accept church doctrine regarding divorce. A substantial proportion of American Catholics are probably only nominal ones and are not very concerned with adherence to doctrines. Since 38.6% of the Catholics in this sample are Mexican-American, it is significant that nominal Catholicism is said to be even more typical of Mexican-American Catholics than of Catholics nationally (Stoddard, 1973; Grebler et al., 1970). Therefore the Catholic youth in this sample may actually represent a broad range of attitudes regarding divorce rather than a single condemnatory one.

It is possible that this broad range of attitudes is typical of non-Catholics as well. In fact, religious affiliation may have little to do with shaping attitudes toward divorce. In support of this idea, several studies have found that Catholic and Protestant divorce rates are very similar (e.g., Christiansen and Barber, 1967; Salisbury, 1964). Assuming that similarities in divorce rates reflect similarities in divorce attitudes, Catholics may actually be no more condemnatory of divorce than are Protestants. Therefore, Catholic and Protestant children's attachment to their parents may be similarly affected by father-absence. The lack of a strong pattern showing father-absence to be more important to Catholics than to Protestants is therefore not inconsistent with the divorce-tolerance framework.

CONCLUSIONS

This study builds upon previous research in showing that the influence of father-absence is different for boys and girls and is important for some offenses but not others. In addition, the evidence shows variations in the association between father-absence and delinquent behavior for Chicanos and Anglos, Catholics and Protestants, and urban and rural residents. In interpreting these findings, we have argued that a critical variable is likely to be the degree of tolerance of divorce that exists in the significant groups in the child's life: the influence of father-absence is likely to be greatest when divorce tolerance is lowest primarily because of weakened parental attachment.

This interpretation has several important implications. First, it provides a reason for the somewhat contradictory findings of recent broken home research. Studies that have identified a weak or even no association between the broken home and delinquent behavior may have inadvertently utilized predominantly divorce-tolerant respondents, while divorce-intolerance may characterize the samples in which the broken home is more strongly associated with delinquent behavior. The findings regarding the relation between father-absence and girls' delinquent behavior in Table 7 clearly demonstrate this point. Based on an urban sample, the broken home would be dismissed as unimportant for nearly all offenses. But based on a rural sample, the broken home would be regarded as a variable of significant importance. Therefore, an important task for future research on the broken home is to specify the social characteristics of the children for whom the broken home has significant behavioral consequences.

The second implication is that changes over time in the strength of the broken home-delinquent behavior relationship may be reasonably explained by changes in the acceptability of divorce. It has been argued that attitudes towards divorce (among other cultural conditions) may have *biased* early twentieth century social scientists in favor of the broken home explanation and later ones against it (Wilkinson, 1974). While this is likely, it is also possible that lower tolerance of divorce caused the broken home to have a much stronger impact on behavior in earlier years than it does today. If the relation between the broken home and delinquent behavior has weakened because of more tolerance of divorce and if in the future divorce is even more tolerated, the importance of the broken home for delinquent behavior may weaken even further.

Finally, the frame of reference provided here is clearly speculative and requires further study. Attitudinal data regarding divorce must be collected to determine (1) if attachment to divorced parents is affected by tolerance of divorce, (2) if children from broken homes are more likely to be delinquent when they are relatively intolerant of divorce, (3) the sources of variations in divorce attitudes (e.g., religion, ethnicity, residence, and (4) if attitudes change over time and influence the strength of the broken home-delinquent behavior relationship.

While the evidence presented here has shown that the simple relation between father-absence and delinquent behavior is fairly weak, this should surprise no one who recognizes that the etiology of delinquent behavior is complex. Because this complexity has generally been ignored in investigations of the broken home, the theoretical significance of the broken home has been overlooked. This study suggests that the broken home need not be viewed as an isolated factor associated with delinquency. Instead, it may well be one of many causal elements explaining control theory's "attachment to parents." Because parental attachment is considered to have a significant impact on delinquent behavior, an important empirical problem is the specification of its causes.

NOTES

1. Studies of the broken home using official records of delinquent behavior have also identified variations in the strength of the association by offense and characteristics of the child. The findings are not reviewed because of obvious problems of interpretation. It is difficult to determine if those variations are the result of differential treatment or of the direct effect of the broken home.

2. On the questionnaire itself, longer descriptions of the offenses were used: (1) "ruin, break or damage someone else's property on purpose" (vandalism), (2) "beat up or hurt someone on purpose" (assault), (3) "take something from a store on purpose without paying for it" (shoplifting), (4) "take someone's car without their permission" (auto theft), (5) "use any marijuana" (marijuana use), (6) "drink any beer, wine or liquor (not counting sips your parents let you have)" (drinking alcohol), (7) "skip school without an excuse" (truancy), (8) "run away from home" (running away).

3. Ideally, the definition of father-absence should be defined still further. In most studies, and in this one as well, children living with their natural mothers and step-fathers (or other father-substitutes) are classified as father-absent along with children living with their natural mothers only. The two types of families should be examined separately, but it is not practical to do so in this study.

4. There is some debate over which term, Chicano or Mexican-American, is preferred by people of Mexican descent living in the United States. Both are used in the literature and are used interchangeably here.

5. The traditional explanation for the stronger association between the broken home and delinquent behavior for girls than for boys relied on sex role socialization differences of a different kind. Toby (1957) argued that since girls are more controlled than boys, girls have greater difficulty adjusting to the reduction in direct control assumed to occur when parents part. Since the validity of this explanation is unknown, the divorce-tolerance explanation is offered as an equally plausible one.

REFERENCES

AUSTIN, R. L. (1978) "Race, father-absence and female delinquency." Criminology 15 (February: 487-504.
BARKER, G. H. and W. T. ADAMS (1961) "The juvenile offender and his family." Social Education 25 (February): 82-84.
CASSIDY, J. P. (1972) "A Catholic view of marital responsibilities," pp. 131-135 in I. R. Stuart and L. E. Abt (eds.) Children of Separation and Divorce. New York: Grossman.
CHILTON, R. J. and G. E. MARKLE (1972) "Family disruption and delinquent conduct: multiple measures and effect of sub-classification." American Sociological Review 37 (February): 93-99.

CHRISTIANSEN, H. and K. BARBER (1967) "Interfaith versus intrafaith marriage in Indiana." Journal of Marriage and the Family 67 (August): 461-469.

DATESMAN, S. K. and F. R. SCARPITTI (1975) "Female delinquency and broken homes: a re-assessment." Criminology 13 (May): 33-55.

DENTLER, R. A. and L. J. MONROE (1961) "Social correlates of early adolescent theft." American Sociological Review 26 (October): 733-743.

EBERSTEIN, I. and W. P. FRISBIE (1976) "Differences in marital instability among Mexican Americans, Blacks and Anglos: 1960 and 1970." Social Problems 23 (June): 609-621.

GLICK, P. and A. J. NORTON (1977) "Marrying, divorcing and living together in the U.S. today." Population Bulletin 32 (October): 2-39.

GOLD, M. (1970) Delinquent Behavior in an American City. Belmont, CA: Brooks/ Cole.

GREBLER, L., J. W. MOORE, and R. GUZMAN (1970) Mexican-American People: The Nation's Second Largest Minority. New York: Free Press.

HENNESSEY, M., P. J. RICHARDS, and R. A. BERK (1978) "Broken homes and middle class delinquency: a reassessment." Criminology 15 (February): 505-527.

HIRSCHI, T. (1969) Causes of Delinquency. Berkeley: Univ. of California Press.

LEVINGER, G. (1965) "Marital cohesiveness and dissolution: an integrative review." Journal of Marriage and the Family 27 (February): 19-28.

MIRANDE, A. (1977) "The Chicano family: a reanalysis of conflicting views." Journal of Marriage and the Family 39 (November): 747-756.

MONAHAN, T. P. (1957a) "Family status and the delinquent child: a reappraisal and some new findings." Social Forces 35 (March): 250-258.

——— (1957b) "The trend in broken homes among delinquent children." Marriage and Family Living 19 (November): 362-365.

MURRILLO, N. (1971) "The Mexican-American family," pp. 97-108 in N. Wagner and M. J. Haug (eds.) Chicanos: Social and Psychological Perspectives. St. Louis: C. V. Mosby.

NYE, F. I. (1958) Family Relationships and Delinquent Behavior, New York: John Wiley.

OFFORD, D. R., N. ABRAMS, N. ALLEN, and M. POUSHINSKY (1979) "Broken homes, parental psychiatric illness and female delinquency." American Journal of Orthopsychiatry 49 (April): 252-264.

ROSEN, L. (1969) "Matriarchy and lower class Negro male delinquency." Social Problems 17 (Fall): 175-189.

RUBEL, A. J. (1970) "The family," pp. 211-224 in J. H. Burma (ed.) Mexican-Americans in the United States: A Reader. Cambridge, MA: Schenkman.

SALISBURY, W. S. (1964) Religion in American Culture. Homewood, IL: Dorsey.

STODDARD, E. R. (1973) Mexican Americans. New York: Random House.

THOMAS, C. W. and C. M. SIEVERDES (1975) "Juvenile court intake: an analysis of discretionary decision-making." Criminology 12 (February): 413-432.

TOBY, J. (1957) "The differential impact of family disorganization." American Sociological Review 22 (October): 505-512.

U.S. Bureau of the Census (1979) "Divorce, child custody, and child support." Current Population Reports (Series P-23, No. 84). Washington, DC: U.S. Government Printing Office.

——— (1978) "Household and family characteristics: March 1977." Current Population Reports (Series P-20, No. 326). Washington, DC: U.S. Government Printing Office.

WILKINSON, K. (1978) "Juvenile delinquency and femininity." Unpublished doctoral dissertation, University of Arizona.

——— (1974) "The broken family and juvenile delinquency: scientific explanation or ideology?" Social Problems 21 (June): 726-739.

WILLIE, C. V. (1967) "The relative contribution of family status and economic status to juvenile delinquency." Social Problems 14 (Winter): 326-335.

Rodney Stark
Daniel P. Doyle
Lori Kent
University of Washington, Seattle

2

REDISCOVERING MORAL COMMUNITIES:
Church Membership and Crime

At least since the time of Emile Durkheim, control theories have been prominent in social science analyses of crime and delinquency. The common element in all forms of control theories is the emphasis on the bonds between the individual and society. When these bonds are strong, the individual is expected to conform to the moral order. But when these bonds are weak, the individual is free to deviate. Social bonds constitute individual stakes in conformity (Weis, 1977; Hirschi, 1969).

Contemporary research has focused on two major kinds of social bonds. It is agreed that deviance can cost us the affection of our friends and relatives (attachments), and make forfeit our present accomplishments and future prospects for success (commitments). A considerable body of data supports the thesis that variations in these social bonds greatly influence deviant behavior (Weis, 1977).

Nevertheless, one of the most central elements in Durkheim's conception of the social bonds has long been missing from modern control theories as well as from the research literature. Durkheim placed *religion* at the center of his conception of the moral order. Indeed, Durkheim's (1915) classic *definition* of religion is a "unified system of beliefs and practices" which unite adherents into a "moral community." Yet, one looks in vain in contemporary theoretical writing on crime and delinquency for much discussion of how religion sanctions the moral order, or for the introduction of religious variables in empirical research.

AUTHORS' NOTE: This research was conducted under the auspices of the Center for the Assessment of Delinquent Behavior and Its Prevention, University of Washington, and was funded under Grant No. 77JN990017 from the National Institute for Juvenile Justice and Delinquency Prevention, Law Enforcement Assistance Administration, U.S. Department of Justice. The granting agency is in no way responsible for analyses or interpretations presented in this chapter.

43

In a recent paper we reestablished the importance of the "lost" relationship between religiousness and delinquency (Stark et al., forthcoming). To do so, however, we had to consider the *social* as well as the individual impact of religiousness on conformity. That is, only in communities where the majority profess religious faith, and thus where religion is an integral part of everyday life, does individual religious commitment limit delinquency. In communities where religion does not receive overt, customary expression, variations in *individual* religiousness do not influence delinquency. That is, in highly secularized communities religion does not bind *even its adherents* to the moral order.

These findings clarified the conflicting empirical results about the relationship between religiousness and delinquency. The intitial studies finding no such relationship were based on data from highly secularized cities on the West Coast (Hirschi and Stark, 1969). Several subsequent studies done elsewhere in the nation found quite robust religious effects on delinquency (Higgins and Albrecht, 1977; Albrecht et al., 1977). Using national data we were able to make the correlations between religiousness and delinquency rise and fall by varying the religious ecology.

In our earlier work, high schools served as the ecological units of analysis. Correlations between religiousness and delinquency rose or fell depending upon the degree to which high schools resembled moral communities (contained a majority of students who were religious). We also found that *levels* of delinquent behavior varied in the same way: the more secularized the school, the higher the proportion of delinquent boys.

In the present study we seek the effects of moral climates on crime rates. Specifically, we use standard metropolitan statistical areas (SMSAs) as our unit of analysis and attempt to demonstrate that variations in their religiousness account for a substantial amount of the variation in their crime rates. If Durkheim was right, SMSAs with high proportions of their populations active in organized religion ought to have lower crime rates.

METROPOLIS AS A MORAL COMMUNITY

Human ecologists have long suspected that the moral integration of cities plays an important role in limiting many kinds of deviance: crime, suicide, alcoholism, mental illness, marital breakups, and the like (Angell, 1974). But they mainly have had to infer this from correlations among these deviance rates. Direct measures of the moral, such as religiousness, have been lacking. The U.S. Census is not permitted to collect data on religious affiliation or participation, while survey studies have lacked sufficient cases to permit characterization of specific cities.

Adequate data recently became available from a privately financed census of the membership of nearly all religious denominations (Johnson et al., 1974).[1] These data made it possible to operationalize the concept of "moral community" in a way directly suitable to Durkheim's definition: the proportion of the population in an SMSA who are united by religion into a "moral community called a Church" (1915: 47).

As we report below, American SMSAs differ extremely in their proportions of church members. This fact has tended to be obscured by the familiar survey research findings that virtually all Americans will claim affiliation with some religious denomination when they are asked "What is your religious affiliation?" But only about half of the U.S. population actually is carried on the membership roles of a specific church. That is, while nearly everyone claims a religion, about half are unchurched. This is not to suggest that the unchurched half of the population is predominantly irreligious. The majority of them also accept common religious beliefs (Stark and Glock, 1968). But the fact that they are not part of an organized religious body suggests that their religion is not very salient and it must certainly be the case that unchurched people receive less systematic reinforcement of their faith. For these reasons we believe that variations in the proportions of church members is an appropriate and direct measure of the religious climate of metropolitan areas.

We readily acknowledge that this measure is not all that we would like. While many unchurched people hold religious beliefs, many churched people are not particularly religious in other ways (Stark and Glock, 1968). Hence it would be especially valuable to have various measures of belief to help portray the religious climate of SMSAs. It would also be desirable to have measures of other aspects of faith: private prayer, scripture reading, and the extent to which religion finds expression in everyday conversations and via the local media. However, since no such data for SMSAs are likely to become available, it is futile to list them. More important, our research on delinquency suggests that if only one measure of religiousness were available it ought to be one that reflects *social* rather than purely individual manifestations of piety. It may well be that a wholly private faith can satisfy the religious needs of many individuals. But our findings suggest such faith will have very slight importance in binding persons to the moral order. Recall that in highly secularized communities we found that even the most intensely religious teenagers were no less likely than the most irreligious to commit delinquent acts. Indeed, in such communities there may not even be any correlation between religiousness and conventional moral values (Hirschi and Stark, 1969). For faith to influence behavior it must do so through creating a moral *climate,* and this requires the social expression of religion. Church membership directly measures the social embodiment of religion.

As mentioned, American metropolitan areas differ immensely in their proportions of church members. We have expressed church membership as the number of members per 1,000 population for each SMSA. In some metropolitan areas the rate exceeds 900 per 1,000. In others it falls well below 300 per 1,000.

RELIGION AND CRIME

Data on crime rates come from the Uniform Crime Report for 1972 (and thus are contemporary with the data on church membership). Deficiencies in the official data made it necessary to omit 24 SMSAs for which only partial crime data were available. We also were forced to omit 26 SMSAs from the New England region because of well-known problems in how they are constituted.[2] Thus our analysis is based on the remaining 193 SMSAs.

An initial test of our hypothesis produced a highly significant correlation of –.36 between the church membership rate and the overall crime rate. However, this correlation was somewhat reduced by an uncontrolled suppressor variable. The proportion of the population that is black is modestly positively related both to the crime rate and to the church membership rate. With this variable controlled the correlation between church membership and crime rises to –.44, which is significant above the .001 level. Moreover, no other variable we examined had so large an effect on the crime rate—and we examined all of the standard variables found to be important in other ecological studies of the crime rate.

The overall crime rate includes seven fundamental crime categories (plus some additional minor property offenses). However, property crimes constitute so large a proportion of the total of indexed crimes that it is wise to examine each of the constituent crime categories separately. As can be seen in Table 2.1, church membership has considerably more impact on property crimes than on violent crimes (–.45 vs. –.20). Moreover, within these categories there is considerable variation in the correlations when more specific offense categories are examined. Thus, among property crimes, high correlations are found for the burglary rate (–.46) and the larceny rate (–.44). But the correlations between church membership and auto theft are much lower (–.18), although still significant above the .05 level.

Among violent crimes, the correlations are significant, but somewhat low, for the homicide rate (–.12), the robbery rate (–.16), and the assault rate (–.14). But the correlation between church membership and the rape rate is quite high (–.41).

It is not novel to discover that variables that influence property crime rates have less effect on crimes of violence, and vice versa (Crutchfield et

TABLE 2.1   Partial Correlation Between Church Membership and
Crime Rates Controlling for the Percentage Black

	Number of Church Members Per 1,000
Official crime rate	−.44*
Subcategories of crime:	
Property crime rate	−.45*
Burglary rate	−.46*
Larceny rate	−.44*
Auto theft rate	−.18**
Violent crime rate	−.20**
Homicide rate	−.12**
Rape rate	−.41*
Robbery rate	−.16**
Assault rate	−.14**
N = 193	

*Significant above .001
**Significant above .05

al, forthcoming). Indeed, these rates are not highly intercorrelated (for
example, the correlation between the larceny rate and the homicide rate in
our data is only .18). This suggests that a major *conceptual* task confronts
criminology. While all of these rates measure "crime," the concept of
crime may be too inclusive to be of utility for theories of crime causation.
Indeed, there is good reason to suppose that these various crimes may have
rather different sources. If so, then we obviously will have to construct
concepts more narrow and more clearly specified than the legal concept of
crime.

In pondering our results, one possible line of interpretation suggests
itself. Homicide and assault tend to be crimes of impulse and to occur
within family and friendship networks. They typically do not reflect a
sustained pattern of deviance (such as a career of burglaries) and thus may
be less easily governed by bonds to the moral order. That is, many who
commit homicide or assault claim they "lost" their heads in the heat of a
dispute, not that they consciously turned their backs on conventional
moral codes. Furthermore, acts of violence that tend to occur within social
networks (rather than between strangers) will tend to be correlated with
community stability—with aspects of communities such as low geographic
mobility that tend to promote contact with family and friends rather than

contact among strangers (Crutchfield et al, forthcoming). However, social forces that sustain community stability also sustain church membership and thus will reduce the impact of religion on these forms of interpersonal violence. We will return to this point.

The impulse versus intentional deviance interpretation is also consistent with the weak correlation between church membership and auto theft. For that offense typically is juvenile "joy riding" and may not signal chronic patterns of nonconformity. Rape, on the other hand, tends to be a repeated offense and should be more symptomatic of sustained nonconformity than are homicide and assault. Moreover, rape is not a network offense, but most typically occurs between strangers. These differences may account for the high negative correlation between church membership and the rape rate.

Unfortunately, this line of reconceptualization is unable to deal with the low correlation between church membership and the robbery rate. Robbery is a career offense and thus indicative of conscious and chronic nonconformity. This would lead us to expect that it would be quite strongly influenced by church membership. Yet, it displays the same weak (but significant) level of correlation as do homicide and assault. We are unable to offer an explanation. Either there is something important about robbery we fail to recognize or our efforts to explain the other variations among crimes are ill-founded.

To test for possible spuriousness a number of other variables were controlled both singly and simultaneously. [3] These included population size, age composition, unemployment, poverty, education, and percent Spanish surname. None of these reduced the initial correlations.

However, one variable did modestly reduce the correlations: population change 1960-1970. This is a somewhat crude measure of in and out migration. In future work we shall demonstrate that high rates of population turnover are a major cause of low church membership rates. Indeed, we hope to show that community instability in the form of rapidly shifting population (including intracity mobility) results in high crime rates because it weakens all forms of primary and secondary relationships which serve to bind people to the moral order. In this sense church membership can be seen as an intervening variable that serves as an important mechanism linking community instability and deviance. Unfortunately, this analysis will have to be based on a very reduced number of SMSAs, since adequate migration data are available only for those larger than 500,000.

CONCLUSION

It would be easy to suppose that had data on the religious makeup of American metropolitan areas been available all along, religion would long ago have been recognized as an important factor in restraining criminal acts. Given this supposition, this chapter is little more than making obvious use of a new opportunity.

But we are not sure that is the case. For one thing, the religion data we used in this chapter have been available for much of the decade and thus a great many other researchers have passed up this easy opportunity. Similarly, our chapter, reestablishing the "lost" relationship between religion and delinquency, was based primarily on secondary analysis of data sets more than ten years old.

We are inclined to think that religion has been omitted from modern research on crime and delinquency for a variety of reasons having little if anything to do with the availability of data.

One of these reasons is the lack of interest in *all sources of conformity* in much current work on deviance. Rather than asking what factors bind persons to conformity, the greatest current effort has gone into asking what factors drive persons to deviate. Those who pursue understanding of how poverty, racism, or capitalism cause crime, or cause acts of "incipient revolution" to be labeled as crime, are not well-positioned to ask how conventional institutions bind people to conform. Indeed, for many recent writers, such institutions are themselves seen as objectionable, as sources of "false consciousness," or at least as old-fashioned. Thus not only religion, but the family and the schools have received less emphasis in recent studies of deviance than might be expected given the size of their known empirical effects.

Another reason for neglect of religion probably stems from the fact that social scientists are a highly irreligious group and that many expect religion to soon disappear (Stark and Bainbridge, forthcoming). Such a view of religion easily is translated into neglect of its social consequences—indeed, into the conclusion that the effects of religion either are negligible or harmful.

Now, there is no reason that social scientists ought to be religious or for them to oppose the secularization of society. However, personal preferences ought not to be so intrusive as to shroud understanding of social phenomena. At the very least, declines in religious commitment ought not be regarded as an unmixed blessing without an assessment of the full range of probable cónsequences. Clearly, secularization entails certain costs. To conclude our chapter we would like to point out a few of these costs.

The data we have examined suggest that nineteenth-century social scientists were correct about the central role played by religion in sustaining the moral order. Cities with higher proportions of church members have lower rates of crime than do more secular cities. Indeed, low church membership rates help explain a very marked regional difference in crime rates. Although it has received remarkably little public notice, the Pacific region has a substantially higher total crime rate than do other parts of the nation. And the Pacific region has by far the lowest church membership rates. Those who would celebrate the low church membership in California, Oregon, Washington, Alaska, and Hawaii as indicative of enlightenment and as a portent of the future must also recognize the probability that this must be paid for in terms of high crime rates.

In other research we report that low church membership is associated with high rates of *religious deviance* (Stark et al., 1979; Stark and Bainbridge, forthcoming). Church membership rates are very strongly negatively correlated with the presence of religious cults and with a variety of occult activities. This also accounts for the high incidence of religious deviance in the Pacific region. With population taken into account this areas has three times as many cults and much higher levels of occult activity than does any other region. Furthermore, data show that a decline in church membership does not reflect a growing population of "enlightened" humanists, agnostics, or atheists. What it reflects are people who still accept the supernatural, but who, lacking an organizational anchorage for their beliefs, engage in a great deal of religious and mystical experimentation and seeking. Hence, religious fads, susceptibility to cynical or demented prophets (such as Jim Jones), and other such phenomena also must count as probably costs of the weakening of traditional religious organizations.

In further work we shall explore the impact of religious commitment on other social problems including drug and alcohol abuse, sexual deviance (recall the high correlation with rape), family instability, school dropout rates, suicide, and the like. We will be very surprised if most of these phenomena are not also markedly influenced by religion.

Such a list of the costs of secularization need not be taken as grounds for supporting organized religion, and surely that is not our intention in pointing them out. But we do believe it is the job of social science to understand how societies actually function. And clearly, it seems to be the case that religion has been, and remains, a potent social fact. To understand just what its effects are, and why they occur, thus remains part of the agenda of a comprehensive social science.

NOTES

1. The omission of Jews and of members of black denominations from the numerators, while all blacks and Jews are placed in the denominators, produced extreme biases in the published rates. The present analysis is based on corrected rates created by an apparently valid estimation procedure (Stark, forthcoming).

2. Some New England states are formed of very large townships rather than counties. In constructing SMSAs in this region the U.S. Census breaks up these units, often assigning different parts of the same township to two different SMSAs. However, the Uniform Crime Report data are available only for these townships as whole units and thus it is impossible to break down the data and assign the proper portions to the different SMSAs. To do so would require the assumption that all parts of a given township have crime rates identical to the township as a whole—which clearly cannot be justified.

3. Partial correlation, rather than regression, is appropriate here because our purpose is not to see how much total variance in the crime rate we can account for. The independent effects of these control variables are not of primary interest, but only the fact that the relationship between church membership and crime is not spurious.

REFERENCES

ALBRECHT, S. L., B. A. CHADWICK, and D. S. ALCORN (1977) "Religiousity and deviance: application of an attitude-behavior contingent consistency model." Journal for the Scientific Study of Religion 3: 263-274.

ANGELL, C. (1974) "The moral integration of American cities. II." American Journal of Sociology 80: 607-629.

CRUTCHFIELD, R., M. GEERKEN, and W. COVE (forthcoming) "Crime rate and geographic mobility."

DURKHEIM, E. (1915) The Elementary Forms of the Religious Life. London: Allen & Unwin.

HIGGINS, P. C., and G. L. ALBRECHT (1977) "Hellfire and delinquency revisited." Social Forces 55: 952-958.

HIRSCHI, T. (1969) Causes of Delinquency. Berkeley: Univ. of California Press.

——— and R. STARK (1969) "Hellfire and delinquency." Social Problems 17: 202-213.

JOHNSON, D. W., P. R. PICARD, and B. QUINN (1974) Churches and Church Membership in the United States. Washington, DC: Glenmary Research Center.

STARK, R. (forthcoming) "Estimating church-membership rates for ecological areas."

———, W. S. BAINBRIDGE, and D. P. DOYLE (1979) "Cults of America: a reconnaissance in space and time." Sociological Analysis.

STARK, R. and W. S. BAINBRIDGE (forthcoming) "Secularization, revival, and cult formation."

STARK, R., L. KENT, and D. P. DOYLE (forthcoming) "Religion and delinquency: the ecology of a 'lost' relationship."

STARK, R. and C. Y. GLOCK (1968) American Piety. Berkeley: Univ. of California Press.

WEIS, J. G. (1977) "Comparative analysis of social control theories of delinquency: the breakdown of adequate social controls." Preventing Delinquency: A Comparative Analysis of Delinquency Prevention Theory. Washington, DC: National Institute for Juvenile Justice and Delinquency Prevention.

Ralph B. Taylor
Stephen D. Gottfredson

Johns Hopkins University

Sidney Brower

*University of Maryland at Baltimore
and
Baltimore City Department of Planning*

THE DEFENSIBILITY OF DEFENSIBLE SPACE:
A Critical Review and a Synthetic
Framework for Future Research

This chapter assesses defensible space theory and research. Conceptual problems with statements of the theory, and methodological problems with the research are examined. For ease of presentation past development of defensible space theory and research is divided into first- and second-generation efforts. In first-generation efforts almost no conceptual attention is given to social predictor or mediating variables. In second-generation efforts more conceptual attention is directed to these social variables.[1] The difference between these two phases is largely one of emphasis. Although a study that we assign "first-generation" status is generally more limited in scope than a "second-generation" study, we do not wish to imply that the first-generation efforts should necessarily be considered less mature or developmentally inferior.

Our assessment of the work in this area leads to rather sobering conclusions. Defensible space theory contains several untested, and in some cases erroneous assumptions. Research to date has suffered from numerous problems, and has only recently tested the full theory. Nonetheless, it is clear that defensible space theory is in a uniquely advan-

AUTHORS' NOTES: We are indebted to Karen Franck for very in-depth comments on an earlier version of this chapter. Tet Motoyama and Herb Rubenstein also commented on an earlier draft. Some of the research described was supported by Grant 78-NI-AX-0134 from the Law Enforcement Assistance Administration, National Institute of Law Enforcement and Criminal Justice, U.S. Department of Justice. Opinions expressed herein are solely our own and do not represent opinions or official policies of the Department of Justice.

tageous position to offer potential solutions to a host of urban residential ills. We propose a revised defensible space theory that is grounded in the context of recent research (Taylor, 1978) and observations (Brower, 1979, 1980) on human territoriality. We view this revised model as a step toward conceptual clarification, which is set within the context of normal science (Kuhn, 1962). It is fueled by an applied, multidisciplinary perspective.

We also report results of a recent effort to test a revised defensible space model in the Baltimore residential environment. Finally, we highlight some areas of ambiguity which need to be resolved.

FIRST-GENERATION DEFENSIBLE SPACE THEORY AND RESEARCH

Theory

Defensible space theory was originated by planners. It was first sketchily outlined by Jacobs (1961). She suggested that to reduce urban residential crime: (a) buildings should be oriented toward the street, thereby encouraging natural surveillance and the "eyes on the street"; (b) public and private domains should be clearly distinguished; and (c) outdoor spaces should be placed in proximity to intensively used areas. Jacobs's ideas were based solely on personal observation and anecdotes. Newman (1973a, 1973b) later elaborated these ideas into defensible space theory.[2] His model suggested that physical design changes could "release latent attitudes in tenants which allow them to assume behavior necessary to the protection of their rights and property" (Newman, 1973b: xii). These behaviors included "a significant policing function, natural to their daily routine and activities," which would "act as important constraints against antisocial behavior" (Newman, 1973b: xii). In short, Newman proposed that design features could encourage territorial cognitions and behaviors on the part of the residents, and that these, in turn, would reduce unwanted intrusions and other criminal behaviors. Graphically, Newman's original model may be portrayed as follows:

Design features (+) Territorial Attitudes and Behaviors (-) Crime and Antisocial Behavior

Newman argued that the focus on design as a key predictor variable was justified. "Our work over the past two years . . . has led us to conclude that the form of the static components of our living environment is, in and of itself, a factor which significantly affects crime rates" (Newman,

1973b: xii). His proposed design ingredients included four major components (Newman, 1973a: 9; 1973b: xv): (a) the use of real and symbolic barriers subdividing the residential environment into manageable zones which would "encourage tenants to assume territorial attitudes and prerogatives"; (b) the provision of opportunities for residential surveillance; (c) the design of sites so that the occupants are not perceived as stigmatized or vulnerable; and (d) the placement of residential structures in proximity to safe or nonthreatening areas.

Four features of the original model are notable. First, design features are treated as predictors of paramount importance. Second, territorial cognitions and behaviors play a critical role in mediating the ultimate impact of design on unwanted intrusions and other antisocial behaviors. Third, design is conceptualized as a releaser or disinhibitor of territorial attitudes and behaviors. Finally, it assumes that the territorial instinct is latent but strong in all residents. This hydraulic, universal view of territoriality had been suggested by Ardrey (1966) and others.

Newman's model is in part compelling due to the context in which it was developed. Rising crime rates in public housing projects and in other urban residential areas were prevalent at that time. The model suggests that a major social problem can be solved through fairly straightforward and specific design solutions.

Research

Newman (1973a) presents a variety of evidence designed to test his model. The empirical studies use archival data on crime in housing projects available from the New York City housing authority. According to the author, the most dramatic empirical support of the theory comes from a comparison of two adjacent housing projects, one which has defensible space characteristics (Brownsville), and one which does not (Van Dyke). Newman suggests that the badly designed project has a higher total number of crime incidents, and higher maintenance costs, and that these differences cannot "be explained away by variations in tenant characteristics in the two projects" (1973a: 49).

To further test the model Newman performed statistical analyses on physical and social characteristics affecting location and frequency of crime in 133 New York City housing projects. He concludes that "the overall results of the analyses of variance coupled with the trend analysis and the regressions, are that relationships between physical design features and crime patterns have been established" (1973a: 234). In support of this conclusion he cites an analysis of variance result which indicated that crime was more frequent in taller buildings.

Newman also cites regression results as support. It is interesting to note that the best predictor of the criterion variable (rate of indoor robberies) is a *social* variable (percent families on welfare, R^2 = .21), and that subsequent physical predictors, in comparison, add less explained variance (R^2 = .16).

Defensible space theory was also tested in a study conducted by the Institute for Community Design Analysis (Kohn et al., 1975). The basic format of the study involved making physical modifications to promote defensible space at two public housing projects (Clason Point and Markham Gardens), (1) conducting before/after measures at these sites, and (2) making comparisons between the modified projects and physically similar but unmodified projects (Cherry Hill and Barry Farms). The modifications at Clason Point and Markham Gardens involved such changes as lighting on paths, fences around yards, wider walks and raised curbing, and establishing play areas.

Results suggested that the modifications did not have a clear-cut effect on mediating such territorial behaviors as gardening and planting. Rather, these behaviors appeared to be annual events that about half the sample in each project engaged in. The authors did note a reduction in fear of crime at Clason Point. Cross-project (i.e., modified vs. unmodified) differences in safety, neighboring activities, and self-reported victimization were observed.

The behavioral, crime-related outcomes of modifications to the projects were not clear-cut. For example, at Clason Point the installation of street lights was concurrent with (1) a *de*crease in crimes between 5 and 9 p.m., (2) an *in*crease in crimes between midnight and 5 a.m., and (3) an *in*crease in total crime. Thus, it appears that the defensible space modifications were not as successful as hoped in deterring crime.

In most of other first-generation studies the researchers attempt to link design features directly to crime-related outcomes. In some studies additional areal-level social predictors are examined. Most studies do not measure mediating territorial cognitions or behaviors.

Bevis and Nutter (1978) conducted block- and tract-level analyses of the relation between type of street layout and residential burglary rate. They found that inaccessible street layouts, i.e., dead end, cul-de-sac, and L-type blocks, were associated with low rates of residential burglary, and that this association could not be explained by traditional social variables. Although this study clearly establishes a link between environmental design and crime rate, the limited range of variables measured makes it unclear whether the results support or contravene defensible space theory.

Inaccessible street layouts may make an area a more manageable. better demarcated zone for residents to control. This in turn, may reduce crime (cf., Appleyard, 1976). On the other hand, since there is less auto and pedestrian traffic in inaccessible streets, there is also less surveillance and use, which, according to the theory, should promote burglary. At this point, we refrain from interpreting this study as either clearly supporting or detracting from defensible space theory. (Frisbie (1978) interprets the study as supporting the theory.)

Pablant and Baxter (1975) explored the relation between school vandalism and environmental attributes. The study is notable in that the impact of adjoining neighborhood features were also considered. In addition, schools were chosen that varied on vandalism rate but were similar in terms of other social variables. The results provided some support and some refutation of defensible space theory. As would be predicted by the theory, schools in neighborhoods with better surveillance opportunities and higher activity patterns had lower vandalism rates. However, in contrast to defensible space predictions, schools with better lighting and fences did *not* experience a lower vandalism rate. One of the strongest findings of the study was that schools that were well-maintained, and aesthetically looked-after, experienced low rates of vandalism.

In his investigation of public and private housing projects, Mawby (1977) found that high-rise projects did *not* exhibit higher offense rates than low-rise projects. He notes: "Newman's theory gains no support from the data" (Mawby, 1977: 173). However, as in Pablant and Baxter (1975), surveillance opportunities were important for crimes against property. Crimes against business property were less likely in areas where there were more potential witnesses.

Brown (1979) investigated the relation between territorial "cues" and the occurrence or nonoccurrence of residential burglary. The cues assessed included real and symbolic barriers, surveillance opportunities, and traces of resident use. Although the physical features explained only a modest portion of outcome variance (16%), the strongest predictor variable was surveillance opportunities (neighboring houses visible). This study, like others, establishes a link, albeit modest, between design and crime.

Tien et al. (1979) evaluated street lighting projects. Limited evidence suggested that improved lighting may reduce fear of crime. Wilson (1978) examined the relation between areal social characteristics, defensible space features, and vandalism, in London housing projects. She found that the best and most consistent predictor of vandalism was the level of child density: higher densities meant more property damage. In low child density locations, physical defensible space features were linked, to some extent, with vandalism rates. The author concludes "this study gave some limited support to Newman's contentions" (1978: 60).

In another study of English housing projects (Clarke, 1979), social composition, level of caretaking, and maintenance were found to be the best predictors of vandalism rates. Modest associations between defensible space features and vandalism rates were revealed.

In an examination of telephone booth vandalism Mayhew et al. (1979) found that the strongest predictor of abuse was tenure type: booths with more public housing nearby were more vandalized. Controlling for tenure type, booths overlooked by more nearby windows were less vandalized.

In sum, this latter group of studies reveals a consistent albeit modest linkage between design features, particularly surveillance opportunities, and crime-related outcomes. However, studies that include social predictors find that these often outperform the physical predictors.

An Appraisal of the Theory and Research

In Newman's initial statement of the theory territorial behavior is treated in a loose, metaphorical fashion. He suggests that territorial behaviors and cognitions are universally latent in all residents and can be released by design features. Newman's treatment of territoriality would seem to be problematic on three counts. First, he fails to define clearly what he means by territoriality, and this has resulted in considerable confusion (Hillier, 1973). Others have followed his example and treated territoriality in a fairly cavalier fashion (Gardiner, 1978). Second, recent research has indicated that it is inappropriate to think of human territoriality as an undifferentiated instinct. Rather, human territoriality is a series of goal-directed, spatially dependent behaviors and cognitions, which operate at various levels of social organization, and foster several aspects of interpersonal functioning (Suttles, 1972; Sundstrom, 1977; Edney, 1976; Taylor, 1978). Third, recent research (e.g., Scheflen, 1971; Suttles, 1968) has indicated that territorial behaviors and cognitions vary widely across subcultural groups. Thus, the impact of design on territoriality is likely to vary widely across these groups. Newman seems to suggest that particular design solutions will be equally effective, and have the same type of impact, in all social and cultural groups or subgroups.

In Newman's initial statement of the theory, design is the main predictor variable. He suggests that design strategies serve as the prime mover, and induce the cognitions and behaviors that lead ultimately to reduced crime. Although such a focus is parsimonious, it is overly restrictive. Research has revealed many determinants of informal social control processes (Wellman and Leighton, 1979).

Finally, Newman's theory contains several behavioral assumptions that may be unwarranted (Mawby, 1977). For example, he assumes that residents are willing to exercise a policing function, and thus would take advantage of surveillance opportunities to watch over local spaces. Assumptions such as these deserve to be directly tested.

There seems to be a substantial conceptual slippage between the theory as stated by Newman, and reported research. The author postulates territorial behaviors and cognitions as crucial variables which mediate the impact of design on crime-related outcomes. However, these intervening variables are not measured in the research; their relationship with the predictors and outcomes is not assessed. In short, Newman's data (1973a) do. not serve as a test of the theory. The results he presents tread dangerously close to architectural determinism (Broady, 1972; Gans, 1968). This is a stance he takes pains to avoid elsewhere. This problem is also evident in first-generation studies conducted by others. Their authors' statements notwithstanding, many of them do not serve as even *limited* tests of defensible space theory.

Kohn et al. (1975) did assess the mediating variables of territorial behaviors and cognitions, as well as crime-related outcomes, in different arenas. However, there is still slippage between the spatial domain of the mediating, and outcome variables. If crimes were reported in a particular location the authors did not attempt to uncover the territorial behaviors or territorial cognitions relevant to that space. Thus it is not clear whether the critical mediating variables, territorial behaviors and cognitions, actually covaried with crime related outcomes. Such findings are needed if defensible space is to be critically tested.

When we focus on the methodological quality of first-generation defensible space research, several problems are apparent. Newman's first-reported research (1973a) and Kohn et al. (1975) both focus on several projects simultaneously. The idea is that if different projects, with varying physical designs, have different crime rates, then the latter can be explained in terms of the former. The logic of this analysis breaks down unless we are assured that *except for design,* the different projects are equal. If the projects differ on other variables besides design then the variation in crime rates may be attributed to these other variables.

As noted above, Newman's most dramatic "proof" of defensible space projects comes from his comparison of two adjacent projects (Newman, 1973a). While he suggests that the two projects are equal on tenant characteristics, his tables suggest that the people moving into each are dissimilar. (Hillier, 1973; see Newman, 1973a: Table B3). Thus, the noted crime and maintenance differences may perhaps be explained in terms of self-selection. In addition, the profile of people moving into each project may be determined in part by the reputation of each site (Mawby, 1977). The same problem of interpreting cross-project differences occurs in Kohn et al. (1975). As noted above, they observed differences between modified and unmodified projects on neighboring activities, safety ratings, and self-reported victimization. Unfortunately, these outcomes may be explained by variables other than the presence or absence of defensible space modifications. The unmodified projects are different from the modified projects in terms of tenant racial and social composition. In addition, the crime rate in the neighborhoods surrounding the various projects may have also been different. Thus, the cross-project differences observed could be explained by social instead of physical variations.

A second problem is that many of these studies use a "modification blitz" approach in which several physical features of the environment are changed at the same time (e.g., Kohn et al., 1975). This makes the interpretation of results problematic. If crime-related outcomes go down, no one knows *which* features are responsible. If crime-related outcomes do not go down, it is possible that the crime reduction due to one feature was canceled out by the crime increase due to *another* feature. Further analytical and methodological problems with Newman's early work are discussed by Patterson (1977: 334-335). These have not recurred in subsequent work.

In sum, first-generation research has established a link between physical defensible space features, particularly surveillance opportunities, and crime-related outcomes. However, this relationship is often overshadowed by links between social variables and crime-related outcomes. The vast majority of studies have failed to assess the territorial cognitions and behaviors, which are postulated as critical mediators of the impact of design. The theory itself suffers on two counts: a misunderstanding and misapplication of human territoriality, and excessive attention to design predictors at the expense of social predictors.

SECOND-GENERATION DEFENSIBLE SPACE THEORY AND RESEARCH

Theory

Second-generation defensible space theory is characterized by increased attention to social predictor and mediating variables. The conceptual implications of various resident and areal characteristics are more fully explored. Residents are important on two counts: as control or policing agents in their own right, and as individuals whose support is needed for the successful implementation of defensible space modifications.

The clearest statement of second-generation theory is found in Newman (1975: 4; emphasis added): "Defensible space is a term used to describe a residential environment whose physical characteristics... function to allow *inhabitants themselves to become the key agents* in ensuring their own security." Thus, the inhabitants' behavior is now "key." As before, the theory suggests that design can "release the latent sense of territoriality and community among inhabitants" (Newman, 1975: 4). Newman asserts that the social variables critical for fostering territoriality are (1) reducing the number of people who share a claim to a space (1975: 55), and (2) grouping residents by uniformity in age and life-style (1975: 74).

The concept of crime prevention through environmental design (CPTED), developed by researchers at Westinghouse (1976, 1977a, 1977b; Lavrakas, Normoyle, and Wagener, 1978) is another version of second-generation defensible space theory. CPTED suggests that in making defensible space alterations it is extremely important to have the support of the local residents and community groups in order that these changes will be viewed in a positive light. Also, CPTED suggests that management be provided to assist residents in selecting and installing target hardening devices, and in making other defensible space changes. The desirability of implementing social defensible space strategies (e.g., improving the neighborhoods' image, encouraging social interaction by residents to promote cohesion and control, increasing community crime prevention awareness) is also noted. The Westinghouse researchers recommend implementing these social and physical changes at the site, block, and neighborhood level.

The Research

CPTED concepts were implemented by Westinghouse at three demonstration sites: a residential neighborhood, a commercial corridor, and a school. At each site local input was received for planning the defensible space modifications. Social modifications (e.g., the organization of local crime-watch groups) were implemented concurrently with physical changes. Although final analyses of all three sites are not yet available, results from the commercial corridor evaluation can be discussed.

The commercial corridor CPTED project in Portland used a variety of physical (e.g., target hardening, more lighting, change traffic patterns) and social (e.g., improve citizen and police response, develop local associations) strategies. Several "hard" outcomes such as residential burglary, commercial burglary, street crime, and commercial robbery were assessed.

The CPTED strategies had little effect on mediating variables (or proximate outcomes), such as pedestrian behavior, perception of risk, social cohesion, or personalization, but they did reduce commercial burg-laries. Time-series analysis indicated fewer commercial burglaries after the CPTED commercial security surveys were carried out (Lavrakas, Normoyle and Szoc, 1978). (A slight but significant decrease in *residential* burglaries was also noted after the *commercial* surveys, although it is difficult to see how these events are related.) Other "hard" outcomes were not affected.

A demonstration project in Hartford sought to implement physical and social defensible space modifications at the neighborhood level. An evalua-tion of this demonstration project has recently been completed by Fowler et al. (1979). They report that when police, resident-based and physical strategies were employed concurrently, residential burglaries decreased, and residents' perceptions of risk were also somewhat reduced. The medi-ating changes a defensible space theorist would expect were also apparent. For example, more residents reported walking in the neighborhood daily, and residents reported that it was easier to recognize outsiders. However, the degree to which these mediating variables actually covaried with the crime-related outcomes was not assessed.

A recent comprehensive assessment of defensible space theory is reported by Newman and Franck (1979). Residents in public housing in three cities were surveyed. The predictor variables included physical, social, and managerial factors. The outcomes included crime, fear of crime, and residential instability. It was expected that major linkages between the predictors and outcomes would be via mediating variables such as resident control and use of space, and interaction patterns. Using the site (n = 63) as the unit of analysis, a multistage causal model was applied to the data. The results largely support the proposed model: strong direct effects of the predictors, and strong indirect effects via the mediating variables were found.

In a study of burglary in Toronto, Waller and Okihiro (1978) found that, in apartments, there was no relationship between territorial control over adjoining spaces and the likelihood of being burglarized. However, levels of social cohesion differentiated burglarized from non-burglarized houses. Also, burglarized houses were less surveillable than non-burglarized houses. These results suggest that crime-deterring features may differ for apartment and single-family sites.

An Appraisal of the Theory and Research

Second-generation defensible space theory seeks to incorporate social predictors, and in this respect represents a vast improvement over first-generation theory. However, the theory as articulated by the CPTED authors, is vague on *what* aspects of the social environment interact with which components of design. The nonspecific focus on social climate stands in stark contrast to the clear focus on the relevant components of the physical environment. Newman and Franck (1979) are clear about the relevant aspects of the social environments.

The criticisms noted above for first-generation theory's treatment of territoriality and sociocultural variation apply also to second-generation theory. The CPTED authors in particular assume that a defensible space strategy which works in one sociocultural context will be equally effective elsewhere (Westinghouse, 1976: 2-10). This assumption has not been supported.

In some second-generation efforts there is still considerable slippage between the theory and research. In some studies where the mediating variables were measured, the degree to which the mediating variables actually covary with the outcomes is not assessed (e.g., Fowler et al., 1979). Failure to assess the mediating-outcome link makes it difficult to appraise the theoretical implications of certain patterns of results. For example, Lavrakas, Normoyle and Wagener (1978) concluded that CPTED strategies had a successful impact on "ultimate" outcomes such as commercial burglary, but not on "proximal" or mediating outcomes such as personalization. Does this mean that the CPTED strategies had direct impacts on distal outcomes such as burglaries? Or, does it mean that CPTED strategies had small effects (i.e., nonsignificant) impacts on several mediating variables, but that these several effects accumulated to yield a significant impact on distal outcomes such as crime? The answer is not clear.

In addition, in several studies the exact links between the predictor and mediating variables are ambiguous. In a typical study (e.g., Lavrakas, Normoyle and Wagener, 1978) several predictors and several mediating processes are examined, and the relationship between these two clusters of variables is only vaguely outlined. An exception to this ambiguity is Newman and Franck (1979).

Several of the second-generation empirical investigations have been demonstration projects. Demonstration projects usually involve only one site, and are, in effect, case studies subject to the limitations associated with this mode of inquiry. In a single site demonstration the qualities of the site vis a vis other potential sites needs to be clearly spelled out, as do the criteria for site selection.

In most of the second-generation demonstration projects, several CPTED strategies have been implemented concurrently. For example, social organizational changes were implemented concurrently with police changes and physical design changes in Lavrakas, Normoyle, and Wagener (1978). As was discussed above, this makes it difficult to assess results: if success occurs, which change is it due to; and, if failure occurs, is it because one strategy was canceling out the other? An exception to this is the Hartford project (Fowler et al., 1979), where an attempt was made to phase in CPTED strategies successively. In Hartford the last strategy phased in, i.e., the physical changes designed to personalize the streets, was pivotal in reducing crime-related outcomes. Nonetheless, successive implementation is not independent implementation: we do not know if the physical changes would have been as effective if they were not preceded by social and policing changes.

These criticisms should be tempered by an understanding of demonstration projects. Their purpose is to demonstrate results in a single site, given a theoretical perspective which is assumed true. The planning of the program is built around this objective. Although an evaluation component is included, analysis is rarely as in-depth as with a research project.

A final method problem that deserves mention is aggregation. Since crime is a rare event, researchers will often aggregate up to the block or neighborhood level, or, in the case of public housing, to the site or project level. Although this aggregation increases variance in the crime measure, it drastically reduces the number of cases in the analysis. This reduction prohibits powerful tests of a large number of variables. A second problem is that these aggregated analyses may tell us about aggregate-level relationships and little about what is happening at the individual level (Robinson, 1950). Third, since individual variation around group means is discarded, aggregate-level picture will be clearer than the actual individual-level picture. Taylor (1980) contains a fuller discussion of aggregation issues related to defensible space research.

SUMMING UP DEFENSIBLE SPACE TO DATE

Our review of the theory and evidence leads us to rather sobering conclusions. First, although defensible space theorizing has improved considerably, further conceptual clarification is needed. The interplay between social and physical elements of the environment deserves closer attention. Second, the impact of varying sociocultural contexts needs to be specifically addressed.[3]

Although research has improved dramatically, there are still problems. In many studies the critical mediating variables have not been measured, or have not been measured adequately. Furthermore, most of the research has been limited to housing projects. Investigations of more typical residential environments have not been widespread. Those studies (e.g., Waller and Ohihiro, 1978) that do assess different types of sites (houses versus apartments) find a different result for each. In addition, it has not yet been determined if potential offenders perceive defensible space features. Although defensible space theory is lacking, and research to date inconclusive, we do not feel that it is appropriate to abandon the ship. Rather, we suggest that defensible space theory can be clarified, and that an updated model may be of use in understanding crime-related outcomes in residential environment.

TOWARD THIRD-GENERATION THEORY AND RESEARCH: PROPOSING A REVISED DEFENSIBLE SPACE MODEL

Further evolution in defensible space theory and research is evident. While it is difficult to pinpoint exactly the shape and scope of this emerging third-generation research, we would like to discuss our approach. Our conceptual framework is grounded in the context of recent research on human territoriality. Human territoriality is an appropriate framework because it is concerned with control over bounded spaces (Altman, 1975; Brower, 1980; Edney, 1976; Patterson, 1978; Sundstrom, 1977; Taylor, 1978). Several corollaries follow from reliance upon the concept of human territoriality.

First, the critical features of the physical environment are signs of defense, signs of appropriation, and signs of incivility (Hunter, 1978). Signs of defense are those symbolic and real barriers, directed toward outsiders, that deter unwanted access. Signs of appropriation are territorial markers indicating that a space is used and cared for. Markers are a well-established aspect of human territoriality (Taylor, 1978). Signs of appropriation convey information to coresidents, and may convey information to potential intruders as well. Signs of incivility are physical and social cues (e.g., litter, groups hanging out on corners) of a disintegration of the underlying social order (Hunter, 1978).

Second, the expression of territorial behaviors and cognitions is conditioned by sociocultural contexts (Scheflen, 1971; Taylor, 1978). The same space may be appropriated, used, and defended in very different ways, depending upon sociocultural variation.

Third, territorial behaviors and cognitions are likely to covary closely (Taylor and Stough, 1978; Taylor and Brooks, 1980). As people feel more proprietary and responsible for a space, they will use, embellish, maintain, and defend it more.

A major tenet of this revised defensible space model is that cultural homogeneity in a neighborhood or on a block facilitates residents' appropriation of semi-public and public spaces.[4] Thus, ceteris paribus, culturally homogeneous groups are more likely to exert territorial control over nearby spaces than heterogeneous groups. Another major tenet of our research is that local social ties (Granovetter, 1973; Wellman and Leighton, 1979) facilitate the development of territorial cognitions, and dominant patterns of territorial behaviors. Finally, our model focuses on a broad range of outcomes, including not only crime, but fear of crime and social nuisances as well.

In short, this model suggests that sociocultural characteristics, design, and social networking determine the strength and breadth of territorial cognitions and behaviors. These proprietary feelings and acts, in turn, are perceived by coresidents and potential intruders. Consequently, a host of crime-related outcomes such as nuisances, fear, and police activity may be dampened.

Several features of the model are noteworthy. First, it is longitudinal and thus may be used to help predict or track events as they unfold over time. Second, the model can be applied at any level of analysis: parcel, block, or neighborhood. It also suggests how cross-level links may occur. Finally, the model connects previous research, which has focused solely on offender behavior (e.g., Brantingham and Brantingham, 1978), with research which has focused solely on resident-based crime prevention behaviors.

Although the full model has not as yet been tested, support for several links in the model comes from a recent Baltimore study (Taylor et al., 1978, 1980; Gottfredson et al., 1979; Brower et al., 1978; Taylor, Gottfredson, Brower, Drain and Dockett, 1980). It appears that: local social networks and perceived homogeneity facilitate the development of stronger territorial cognitions and behaviors; strong territoriality, at the block and neighborhood level, dampens crime and fear of crime; and defensible space features signs of appropriation, and signs of incivility covary with crime-related outcomes. Of course, this model is still in the process of being refined and tested. It will be some time before any particular third-generation model is substantiated.

A LOOK AHEAD

Some important issues that must be resolved in future research are listed below, although not in order of importance:

(1) What happens when offenders or potential offenders confront territorial residents, signs of appropriation, or other resident-based features that have a deterrent value? We know a lot about criminal behavior (e.g., Capone and Nichols, 1976), a lot about resident-based behaviors and the residential environment, but not much

about the interface of the two. This issue has received only very passing attention (Brantingham and Brantingham, 1978), and needs to be explored.

(2) Over time, how do offender behaviors affect territorial behaviors and cognitions? Does threat lead people to become more territorial (e.g., Brower, 1980), or less territorial, and does threat influence different people differently?

(3) Is a policing function "natural" to residents? Will residents utilize defensible space features, or stand behind them, and if so, under what circumstances?

(4) What is the cost effectiveness of defensible space as compared to other strategies such as environmental managers (Brower et al., 1976)? Waller and Okihiro (1978) note that defensible space modifications are often costly, and Mayhew (1979) points out that they are irreversible. More thorough comparisons of the advantages and disadvantages of defensible space vis-à-vis other strategies are needed.

(5) How, if at all, do defensible space processes operate in different types of environments (projects versus apartments versus single family dwellings), and what relationships appear consistently in these different settings?

(6) What are the relations among areal context, immediate environment, and individual-level territorial functioning? In the residential environment does the neighborhood determine block functioning, and is, in turn, individual functioning a simple mirror of block dynamics? Or does the process work in the opposite direction, in a "grassroots" fashion? What are the links between a person and the block climate, and how does this vary in different areas?

Crime, fear of crime, and social nuisances in the residential environment are sociospatial problems. They result from a complex mix of factors. Many of these factors are nested in the local environment: residents' attitudes, use patterns, and interaction patterns; and the design of the environment itself. Defensible space theory, if carefully conceptualized and tested, is in a uniquely advantageous position to address these issues. Although defensible space theory, is not fully established, it is most certainly defensible.

NOTES

1. Others (cf., Mayhew, 1979) have also noted a shift, at least in the theory, over time.

2. Defensible space is not only a theory of residential design and crime, it is also a range of mechanisms for environmental control, and the resulting safe environment (Newman, 1973a: 3). The focus of this paper is largely on defensible space as a theory. Waller and Okihiro (1978) have argued that Newman's ideas do not qualify as a theory, but should instead be treated as a heuristic. Nonetheless, Newman does discuss several variables and the relationships between them. This discussion therefore qualifies as a model, which is an early stage of theory development. Thus, we refer to defensible space theory.

3. Our conclusions regarding defensible space theory and research are quite different from those of Rouse and Rubenstein (1978), who stated, "[Newman's] works have been lauded for their theoretical discussion of physical-social phenomena" and "each of these [Newman's] research efforts conducted over the past five years has contributed support for Newman's defensible space theories" (69, 70).

4. After proposing this tenet, we were encouraged to find it was shared by Newman (1975).

REFERENCES

ALTMAN, I. (1975) The Environment and Social Behavior. Monterey, CA: Brooks/ Cole.

APPLEYARD, D. (1976) Livable Urban Streets: Managing Auto Traffic in Neighborhoods. Washington, DC: U.S. Government Printing Office.

ARDREY, R. (1966) The Territorial Imperative. New York: Atheneum.

BEVIS, C., and J. B. NUTTER (1977) "Changing street layouts to reduce residential burglary." Presented at the American Society of Criminology, Atlanta, November.

BRANTINGHAM, P. J. and P. L. BRANTINGHAM (1978) "A theoretical model of crime-site selection," in M. D. Krohn and R. L. Akers (eds.) Crime, Law, and Sanctions: Theoretical Perspectives. Beverly Hills: Sage Publications.

BROADY, M. (1972) "Social theory in architectural design," in R. Gutman (ed.) People and Buildings. New York: Basic Books.

BROWER, S. (1980) "Territory in Urban Settings," in I. Altman, G. Rapoport, and J. Wohlwill (eds.) Human Behavior and Environment. New York: Plenum.

——— (1979) "The design of neighborhood parks." JSAS Catalog of Selected Documents in Psychology 9, 29 (MS 1843).

———, R. R. STOUGH, B. HEADLEY, and L. GRAY (1976) "The design of open space for residential management," in P. Suedfeld and J. A. Russell (eds.) The Behavioral Basis of Design, I. Stroudsburgh, PA: Dowden, Hutchinson & Ross.

BROWER, S., R. B. TAYLOR, S. D. GOTTFREDSON, and K. DOCKETT (1979) "Informal control in neighborhood spaces: The influence of physical features." Presented at the annual meeting of the American Planning Association, Baltimore, October.

BROWN, B. B. (1979) "Territoriality and residential burglary." Presented at the American Psychological Association, New York City, September.

CAPONE, D. L. and W. W. NICHOLS (1976) "Urban structure and criminal mobility." American Behavioral Scientist 20: 199-213.

CLARKE, R.V.G. (1978) "Defensible space and vandalism: the lessons from some recent British studies," in Stadtebau und Kriminalamt (Urban Planning and Crime): Papers of an International Symposium. Bundeskriminalamt, Federal Republic of Germany.

EDNEY, J. J. (1976) "Human territoriality: Comment on functional properties." Environment and Behavior 8: 31-57.

FOWLER, F. J., M. E. McCALLA, and T. W. MANGIONE (n.d.) Reducing Residential Crime and Fear: The Hartford Neighborhood Crime Prevention Program. Washington, DC: U.S. Government Printing Office.

FRISBIE, D. W. (1978) Crime in Minneapolis. Minneapolis: Minnesota Crime Prevention Center.

GANS, H. J. (1968) "Urban vitality and the fallacy of physical determinism," in H. J. Gans, People and Plans. New York: Basic Books.

GARDINER, R. A. (1978) Design for Safe Neighborhoods. Washington, DC: U.S. Government Printing Office.

GOTTFREDSON, S. D., S. BROWER, and R. B. TAYLOR (1979) "Design, social networks and human territoriality: predicting crime-related and social control outcomes." Presented at the annual meeting of the American Psychological Association, New York, September.

GRANOVETTER, M. S. (1973) "The strength of weak ties." American Journal of Sociology, 78: 1360-1380.

HILLIER, B. (1973) "In defense of space." RIBA Journal: 539-544.

HUNTER, A. (1978) "Symbols of incivility: Social disorder and fear of crime in urban neighborhoods." Presented at the annual meeting of the American Society of Criminology, Dallas, November.

Institute for Community Design Analysis (1974) Measuring the Effectiveness of Project Modifications: A Test of Defensible Space Hypotheses. Unpublished manuscript.

JACOBS, J. (1961) The Death and Life of Great American Cities. New York: Vintage.

KOHN, I. R., K. A. FRANCK, and A. S. FOX (1975) "Defensible space modifications in row-house communities." New York: Institute for Community Design Analysis. Unpublished final report.

KUHN, T. S. (1962) The Structure of Scientific Revolutions. Chicago: Univ. of Chicago Press.

LAVRAKAS, P. J., J. NORMOYLE, and R. SZOC (1978) "Commercial security surveys and burglary reduction: a time-series analysis." Presented at the Second National Workshop on Criminal Justice Evaluation. Washington, November.

LAVRAKAS, P. J., J. NORMOYLE, and J. J. WAGENER (1978) "CPTED commercial demonstration evaluation report" (draft). Evanston, IL: Westinghouse Electric Corporation.

MAWBY, R. I. (1977) "Defensible space: a theoretical and empirical appraisal." Urban Studies 14: 169-179.

MAYHEW, P. (1979) "Defensible space: The current status of a crime prevention theory." Howard Journal of Penology and Crime Prevention, 18: 150-159.

———, R.V.G. CLARKE, J. N. BURROWS, J. M. HOUGH, and S.W.C. WINCHESTER (1979) Crime in Public View. London: Her Majesty's Stationery Office.

NEWMAN, O. (1975) Design Guidelines for Creating Defensible Space. Washington, DC: U.S. Government Printing Office.

––– (1973a) Defensible Space: Crime Prevention Through Urban Design. New York: Macmillan.

––– (1973b) Architectural Design for Crime Prevention. Washington, DC: U.S. Government Printing Office.

––– and K. FRANCK (1979) "Factors influencing crime and instability in urban housing developments." Draft executive summary. New York: Institute for Community Design Analysis.

PABLANT, P. and J. C. BAXTER (1975) "Environmental correlates of school vandalism." Journal of the American Institute of Planners: 270-277.

PATTERSON, A. H. (1977) "Methodological developments in environment-behavioral research," in D. Stokols (ed.) Perspectives on Environment and Behavior. Monterey, CA: Brooks/Cole.

ROBINSON, W. S. (1950) "Ecological correlations and the behaviors of individuals." American Sociological Review 15: 351-357.

ROUSE, W. V. and H. RUBINSTEIN (1978) Crime in Public Housing: A Review of Major Issues and Selected Crime Reduction Strategies, Volume I. Washington, DC: U.S. Government Printing Office.

SCHEFLEN, A. E. (1971) "Living space in an urban ghetto." Family Process 10: 429-450.

SUNDSTROM, E. (1977) "Interpersonal behavior and the physical environment," in L. Wrightsman, Social Psychology. Monterey, CA: Brooks/Cole.

SUTTLES, G. D. (1972) The Social Construction of Communities. Chicago: Univ. of Chicago Press.

––– (1968) The Social Order of the Slum. Chicago: Univ. of Chicago Press.

TAYLOR, R. B. (1980) "People on a block in a neighborhood: theoretical and statistical implications of grouped data for community crime prevention research and evaluation." Unpublished manuscript, Johns Hopkins University.

––– (1978) "Human territoriality: a review and a model for future research." Cornell Journal of Social Relations 13: 125-151.

––– and D. K. BROOKS (forthcoming) "Temporary territories: responses to intrusions in a public setting." Journal of Population.

TAYLOR, R. B., S. D. GOTTFREDSON, and S. BROWER. (1980) "Neighborhoods, social networks, and territorial cognitions: threat and control in the urban residential environment." To be presented at the annual meeting of the American Psychological Association, Montreal, September.

––– (1978) "Urban territoriality and crime in residential settings." Environmental Psychology and Nonverbal Behavior 3: 121-122.

–––, W. DRAIN, and K. DOCKETT (1980) "Toward a resident-based model of community crime prevention: Urban territoriality, social networks, and design." JSAS Catalog of Selected Documents in Psychology 10: 39-40 (MS. 2044).

TAYLOR, R. B. and R. STOUGH (1978) "Territorial cognition: assessing Altman's typology." Journal of Personality and Social Psychology 36: 418-423.

TIEN, J. M., V. F. O'DONNELL, A. BARNETT, and P. B. MIRCHANDANI (1979) Street Lighting Projects. Washington, DC: Department of Justice.

WALLER, I. and N. OKIHIRO (1978) Burglary: The Victim and the Public. Toronto: Univ. of Toronto Press.

WELLMAN, B. and B. LEIGHTON (1979) "Networks, neighborhoods and communities: approaches to the study of the community question." Urban Affairs Quarterly 14: 363-390.

Westinghouse Electric Corporation (1977a) Crime Prevention Through Environmental Design. CPTED Program Manual, Vol. 1: Planning and Implementation Manual. Arlington, VA.

——— (1977b) Crime Prevention Through Environmental Design. CPTED Program Manual, Vol. 2: CPTED Strategies and Directives Manual. Arlington, VA.

——— (1976) Crime Prevention Through Environmental Design. Residential Demonstration Plan. Minneapolis, Minnesota. Arlington, VA.

WILSON, S. (1978) "Vandalism and 'defensible space' on London housing estates," in R.V.G. Clarke (ed.) Tackling Vandalism. London: Her Majesty's Stationery Office.

G. R. Patterson

Oregon Social Learning Center, Eugene

4

CHILDREN WHO STEAL

In the end then, control theory remains what it has always been: a theory in which deviation is not problematic. The question 'why do they do it?' is simply not the question the theory is designed to answer. The question is, 'why don't we do it?' There is much evidence that we would if we dared [Hirschi, 1969: 34].

This discussion outlines a general formulation about young children who steal.[1] The formulation is a base from which social learning and social control theories might be compared. But, the primary purpose is to provide a means of integrating the series of empirical analyses relating to this problem being carried out at the Oregon Social Learning Center.

Hirschi (1969) traced the curious stance taken by the social sciences—sociology and psychology alike—that conformity to society's rules and procedures is to be *expected,* while deviance is to be *explained.* The general position assumes that children and adults are moral beings, aware of society's rules and expectations, and that, under normal conditions, they desire to conform to these rules. Internalizing the norms has become a matter of primary concern for theorists in sociology, developmental psychology, and personality theory. The strain theorists would assume that the bond forming the basis for internalization has occurred. The knowledge is also present; but motivational factors, such as extreme deprivation or frustration, cause a disruption in this structure. This disruption leads, in turn, to deviant acts. The cultural deviance theorists, on the other hand, would assume that the norms and rules internalized represent a deviant subset of the culture to which the individual belongs. From this perspective, the individual is conforming, but to deviant norms.

AUTHOR'S NOTE: The author's address is Oregon Social Learning Center, 220 East 11th, Eugene, Oregon 97401. The Center is an affiliate of the Wright Institute in Berkeley, California.

The control theorists, on the other hand, assume that the original attachment or bond may not have developed; that necessary controls were *never internalized*. Lacking such controls, one can expect the child or adult to act out as a matter of course. This position characterizes recent developments in social learning theory as well (Bandura, 1973; Patterson, forthcoming). The most coherent statement of the control theory position, together with a modest empirical foundation, was provided by Hirschi (1969). His updating of the control system postulates an attachment or bond of the normal child to his parents, who, in turn, embody cultural expectations and norms. Given that the attachment or bond exists, this increases the likelihood that the child will be committed to investing time and energy in society's goals. He will also be involved in the activities, such as school and work, that will fulfill these goals. One could expect certain cognitive concommitants of this process that would, in turn, be measurable, such as the belief and value system held by the young person. The attachment or bond is a necessary, but not sufficient condition, for conformity. The accompanying commitment, involvement, and belief systems are also necessary but not sufficient. The general stance is certainly reminiscent of the current developments in cognitive social learning theory as presented by Mahoney (1974). Given a deviant child, both positions might proceed to re-establish the bond of the child to parents; and thus to society. This, of course, has been an implicit goal of psychotherapists in working with delinquent. youths. The impact of the relation between youth and therapist will generalize to establishing again the bonds between the youth and other adults. The second implication is that one could perhaps directly train the child to monitor his own behavior. He might compare acts he has performed or intends to perform against his own set of standards and even to provide consequences for deviations from these norms. This is the goal for the newer developments in behavioral modification as presented by such writers as Mahoney (1974) and Meichenbaum (1977).

BACKGROUND

During the past ten years, the Oregon Social Learning Center has been deeply immersed in the problems of treating several hundred families of young, antisocial children. In the last two years, the effort has been expanded to include chronic delinquent children. This process continues and has led us to some assumptions that are related both to control theories and to traditional social learning viewpoints. For heuristic purposes, we have elected to make some simplifying assumptions about what is involved in deviant behavior. It is not believed that these premises will provide the base from which one may understand the entire spectrum of deviant or delinquent acts. They are, however, a vehicle for initiating efforts to provide a stronger empirical base for what is understood. The empirical base has two components. On the one hand, the staff invests an enormous amount of time in helping families to change the behavior of the delinquent, chronic offender (Reid et al., 1980). Efforts to change these chronic offenders color the hypotheses we entertain. Our perceptions are further influenced by the intensive assessment procedures employed, such as observation in the home, parental daily report measures, and laboratory procedures to augment the traditional emphasis on self-report as a primary data source.

The first hypothesis is that antisocial children maximize their short-term payoffs, and are largely ignoring the long-term consequences for their acts. In the short-term, there is much to be gained by applying pain control techniques to alter the behavior of another person, such as a family member, a peer, a teacher, or a probation officer. Antisocial children train their parents. Antisocial behavior typically has an impact; it is very effective in training adults and peers to cease making demands. The child does not have to do chores nor conform to house rules. Similar techniques are used by the child to train teachers and adults to believe that it is not necessary for that child to go to school or to achieve a reasonable level if he or she does attend.

The second hypothesis is that acts of vandalism and stealing constitute a kind of short-term payoff, which has been characterized as "kicks" or excitement. This position has been elaborated in detail by Patterson (1979, forthcoming a, b) under the rubric of coercion process. It is, of course, necessary to establish that the antisocial and antiproperty deviant acts are, in fact, reinforcing. To date, only the former hypothesis—that antisocial deviant acts are reinforcing—has even a modest empirical base. When stated in reinforcement language, this position is similar to that assumed by the sociological control theorists such as Nye, who explains that "general behavior described as delinquent or criminal need not be explained in any positive sense, since it usually results in quicker and easier achievement of goals than the normative behavior" (1958: 5).

In that context, two- and three-year-old children commit frequent "crimes against property." All two- and three-year-old children take things that belong to other members of the family. They want a cookie, so they take one; they want a toy, so they take it even though it belongs to a brother. School age children steal at least once in their lives. The studies on preschool aggression reviewed by Hartup (1977) showed, in one instance, that 78% of the conflicts involving two- and three-year-old children focused on possession. That is, one child wanted a toy or an object being used by another and simply took it. Some children are simply allowed to continue stealing, which was age-appropriate to preschool children (and not then labeled). Presumably, the children engage in increasingly high rates of stealing first from families and perhaps in the neighborhood, but eventually in school as well. When these rates reach an unacceptable level, the child is then labeled deviant by professionals or agency staff.

The perspective provided by coercion theory introduces a third hypothesis that perhaps differentiates the position somewhat from that of the control theorists. The concept is labeled "arrested socialization." In attacks against people, the assumption is that this behavior occurs at the highest rate for two-year-old children followed by lower rates for three- and four-year-old children. In the study by Patterson (forthcoming a), the mean rate of aversive behavior per minute for normal two- to four-year-old children was .73 responses per minute; for five- to six-year-old children the rate was .42; and for seven- and eight-year-old children it was .21. At the same time, the observed rates of aversive behavior for eight-year-old *problem* children referred for treatment were virtually identical to those for normal two- to four-year-olds! In effect, the identified agressive child was performing behavior at roughly the same rate found for normal preschool children in their culture. The socially agressive child was not performing "deviant" acts; rather he was simply performing behavior acceptable in two- to three-year-old children.

The fourth hypothesis is that more extreme physical violence is an outcome of an escalation involving rather innocuous aversive behavior commonly found in family interaction. Under certain conditions, minor arguments can escalate, over time, to produce physical assaults by otherwise nonaggressive persons.

The fifth assumption concerns the means by which a child is taught to reduce the level of his or her deviant behavior. Children do not outgrow extreme antisocial behavior; they remain deviant unless they are punished. One might consider two courses of action; indeed, both have been emphasized in the social learning literature. One might concentrate on developing in the child a higher order of prosocial skills. Rather than taking an object from another child, we might teach the child to play cooperatively. Rather than hitting another child during a disagreement, we might teach the child to discuss altercations. Rather than stealing something from a parent, we might teach him the virtues of the Protestant ethic regarding work, wages, and salaries. Certainly in the mid-1960s, it was the fond hope of social learning theorists that if competent social behavior was taught, then the deviant behavior such as attacks, hitting, and stealing might wither on the vine. *Unfortunately, there are a series of studies now that show this not to be the case. While it is possible to teach prosocial behavior, success is not accompanied by reductions in aversive attacks on other persons, at least by extremely agressive children.* These studies have been reviewed by Patterson (forthcoming a).

These findings, plus our clinical experience in treating these families, led us to the reluctant conclusion that what is necessary is that the family directly punish, nonphysically, the deviant acts and concentrate on teaching prosocial competing responses. It is ironic that Thomas Hobbes arrived at this position some centuries earlier in *The Leviathan:* "Of all passions, that inclineth men least to break the law is fear. Nay, excepting some generous natures, it is the only thing when there is an appearance of profit or pleasure by breaking the laws that make men keep them" (Hirschi, 1969: 5). This somewhat misanthropic viewpoint implies that delinquent behavior is the responsibility of the immediate social system; that is, the family. It becomes their task to monitor the child's behavior, and when and if the child is delinquent to also accept responsibility for providing an aversive consequence; all of this in addition to teaching the child prosocial skills he also needs to survive. This emphasized here because the focal point of treatment, and the point at which failure is most likely to occur, is in supporting the parents for accepting these two responsibilities: To the extent that parents are able to do this, the offense rates for the chronic delinquent child will be reduced. In effect, nonviolent, nonphysical punishments such as work details are, as treatment, an effective means of reducing rates of delinquent acts. The delicate problems involved in actually teaching nonviolent forms of punishment and other problem-solving skills are outlined in Patterson et al. (1975).

Two Progressions Relating to Deviancy

Labeling an adolescent a chronic delinquent is the outcome of an extended process. In the case of delinquent behavior, this process may be discernible by the age of eight or nine. As viewed here, there are two components. It is assumed that, on the one hand, *there is an accumulating deficit in social skills and competencies.* At each of the critical, developmental stages, the to-be-labeled child is inadequately socialized. The larger the number of these omitted skills, the more likely the child is to be labeled and the more ominous the prognosis for eventual adjustment as a young adult. *The second component describes the pattern(s) of deviancy and the rate it is practiced.* Most families will tolerate some forms of deviancy but not others. In a sense, one might say that the normal family tolerates very low deviancy in any of the antisocial patterns. Within a particular pattern, the more extreme form of the deviant behavior is thought to occur at lower rates, but the relation between high- and low-base rate deviant behavior is transitive. That is, if a child is permitted to perform the more extreme deviant low-base rate event, the child is also to be given permission to perform all of the higher base rate events within that pattern. Again, the implication is that the further the child progresses into this pattern, the more extreme the behavior, and the more likely the label of deviant.

The eventual adjustment as an adult is predicted by the extent to which the child drifts along the two dimensions of skill deficits and antisocial deviancy. The prognosis is the worst for the young boy who is extremely antisocial *and* has extreme deficits in work, peer relations, and self-management (Patterson, forthcoming a).

TYPES OF ANTISOCIAL BEHAVIOR

Within coercion theory, there are two major forms of juvenile antisocial behavior. Each is related to different facets of family process. Each has different implications for later adjustment as a young adult. Each family molds and shapes the child to its own standards. The parents determine what is an acceptable rate of deviant behavior; they also determine which antisocial patterns, if any, are acceptable. The basis for the analysis of these patterns was the parents' identification of problem behavior. This was obtained during the intake interviews with families of antisocial children referred for treatment. A standardized list of 53 complaints was used. These checklists described the kind of symptom behavior for which children ordinarily were referred to child guidance clinics. In the early 1970s, the list of problems was changed to include a list of 31 types of behavior typically found for samples of antisocial boys. During the interview, the parents were asked about each of the items on the list. A Guttman scalogram analysis of various patterns of these intake symptoms produced three progressions (Patterson, forthcoming c). The analysis produced reproducibility coefficients in the .85 to .95 range. Each was replicated at least once. As shown in Figure 4.1, all of the progressions center (begin) on the problem behavior "Noncomply." In some families, the accepted pattern was Immaturity, which proceeded from Noncomply to Whine to Yell to Bedwetting. Other families of problem children did not permit these particular problems to occur; they instead permitted a

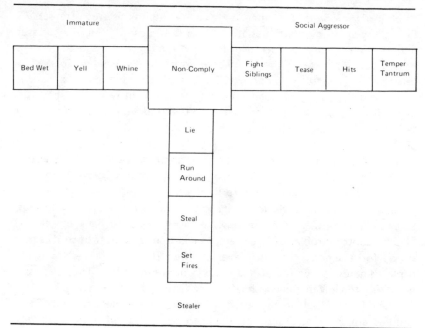

FIGURE 4.1: Some Deviancy Progressions (from Patterson, forthcoming a)

pattern labeled Social Aggressor. The progression here was from Non-comply to Fighting with Siblings to Teasing, to Hitting, and to Temper Tantrums.

The progression of greatest interest was that labeled "Stealer." The parents describe these children as being disobedient; they lie, run around, steal, and set fires. All children who set fires also steal and perform all of the other higher rate problem behaviors as well. The implications for treatment are also straightforward. That is, if the parents can be supported while they train the child to obey and to stop running around, that may reduce the rates of stealing and firesetting.

The Social Aggressor and the Stealer patterns were differentially related to the likelihood of police contacts for nonstatus and status offenses. Moore et al. (1979) analyzed the community follow-up data for a sample of young Stealers who were, on the average, 8.4 years of age. Children who were 14 years of age or older, and who had terminated their contacts with the program for a minimum of two years, composed the follow-up samples: by that time, 84% of the Stealers had at least one police contact, while 24% of the Social Aggressors, and 21% of the Normal sample had at least one police contact. Furthermore, 67% of the Stealers were now chronic offenders; that is, they had four or more nonstatus offenses. As the follow-up study continues, the 17- and 18-year-old Social Aggressor may turn out to be the assaultive delinquent; but that remains to be seen. *As the data now stand, they implicate young, preadolescent Stealers as being at risk for later delinquency.* The qualification that must be made is that it was the younger Stealers *referred for treatment* who were shown to be at risk. Would the prognosis for nonreferred young Stealers be the same? That remains to be established; a longitudinal study is now being planned.

Table 4.1 summarizes the areas of social competence in which antisocial children are deficient. The items on the list were suggested more by empirical findings in the literature than any coherent theory about competency. The studies reviewed in Patterson (forthcoming a) showed that, at early ages, antisocial children were more likely to have bowel and bladder control problems. There are, in addition, a number of studies that show, for example, that antisocial children perceive themselves to be hapless figures, blown hither and yon by the winds of fate. They also tend negatively to view themselves, their peers, family, and other victims.

Their lack of skill in the world of work are well documented. These childred are, at an early age, less likely to do chores, *simply because they have trained their parents to believe that it is impossible. They consistently test low on both achievement and IQ tests.* They more frequently engage in truancy and are more likely to drop out of school. These children are not popular; rather, it is they who are most likely to be rejected by the peer group. It is thought, too, (although no studies are yet available that demonstrate this) that they will fail to develop the skills *necessary to initiate and maintain an intimate relationship with people of either sex.* A failure on these three dimensions would seem, on the face of it, to have ominous implications for later adjustment as an adult. At present, the relation between these early precursors and later adult adjustment is correlational and retrospective.

PARENTING SKILLS: A SET OF FORGOTTEN VARIABLES

The assumption made by most personality theorists is that parenting skills may be taken for granted. Presumably, the information and skill required to bring up a normal child is a part of the conventional wisdom within our culture. These theorists assume that appropriate information is available to all young parents, and that appropriate models and support systems are also available. The author accepts none of these: On the

TABLE 4.1   Skill Deficits in Drift Toward Delinquency

	Self Help	Work	Intimacy
Preschool	1. Bowel and bladder control		1. Share 2. Cooperative play
School age	2. A sense of control over what happens to self	1. Chores 2. Attend school regularly 3. Completes homework assignments 4. Attend 5. Study skills	3. Skills in games 4. Accepted by peers 5. Social skills
	3. Perceive self, mother, father and peers in positive vein	6. Part-time job for money	6. Intimacy

contrary, increasing numbers of young parents function in isolated family systems, removed from modeling influences, informational sources, and support systems. Such being the case, then there will be wide variations among parents in performing parenting skills. Parenting skills describe a perfectly mundane set of operations that would include: (a) *notice what the child is doing;* (b) *monitor it over long periods;* (c) *model social skill behavior;* (d) *clearly state house rules;* (e) *consistently provide sane punishments for transgressions;* (f) *provide reinforcement for conformity;* and (g) *negotiate disagreements so that conflicts and crises do not escalate.*

Most theorists also focus on the child's attachment to the parent. The assumption, of course, is that there is a unilateral effect of the parent on the child. It is equally reasonable to assume that there are marked variations in the *attachment of the parent to the child.* Some of this may be due to the fact that some children are more difficult to care for. The first 50 families of antisocial children treated at the Oregon Social Learning Center showed therapists that many of these parents did not identify with the role of parent *and were not attached to their children. It was, therefore, extremely difficult to teach them to be more effective parents.* In short, from the perspective of coercion theory, neither the parents' motivation nor skills are thought to be a given.

If the variables describing parenting skills occupy the central niche ascribed to them, then they should effectively differentiate the parenting skills applied to out-of-control children from those applied to normal children, and they should further differentiate parenting skills for children who steal from those for socially aggressive children. The data that follow relate to these issues.

Parent Perception

Coercion theory assumes that persons living or interacting closely with deviant individuals eventually alter what they think of as "deviancy." Parents eventually change the definition of deviant behavior. This misclassification characterizes parents of socially aggressive children and parents of children who steal. But one misclassifies examplars of interpersonal aggression, while the other misclassifies examplars of theft.

This difference was first brought to our attention in our efforts to treat children who steal. Many of the parents maintained that since they had never actually seen their child steal, they could not prove that their child had stolen, and therefore could not punish the child (Reid and Patterson, 1976). In numerous instances, someone else had actually *seen* the child steal, but the child's "story" would be accepted by the parents, who would then rise to the child's defense and accuse others of picking on the child. As the parents used the word "steal," it could be used as a label only if it could be *proven,* which was usually impossible; ergo the child did not really steal, ergo no punishment could be applied. There were many variations in this theme. Incidentally, to treat these families, it was necessary to change the labeling process so that it became the child's responsibility to avoid being accused: If the child *was* accused, he or she was then to be punished.

One piece of data consistent with these ideas is from a self-report questionnaire administered to 13 mothers of socially aggressive children and 15 mothers of children who steal. The statistical analysis of these small samples show significant differences on MMPI profiles. The mothers of socially aggressive children were, in general, more anxious, depressed, and generally neurotic. The mothers of children who steal had a MMPI profile that reproduces that obtained by Hathaway and Monachesi (1953) for the adolescent delinquent girl. One suspects the mothers' prolonged interactions with the abrasive, socially aggressive children produces their anxiety and depression. One may also assume that the mother of the child who steals shares the general values, orientations, and perceptions of the delinquent adolescent girl—a set of values held prior to the birth of her own children.

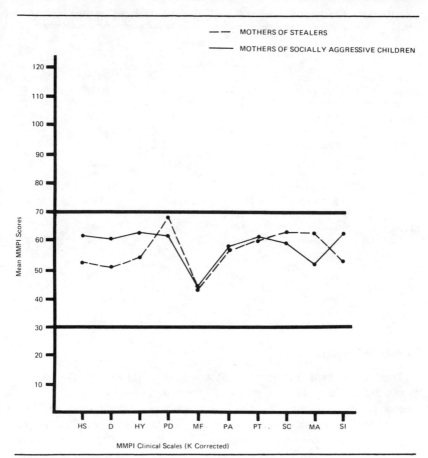

FIGURE 4.2:   MMPI Profiles for Mothers of Stealers and Mothers of Social
Aggressors (from Patterson, forthcoming b)

The implications of these formulations for the child who steals are clear. Following the general tenets of social learning theory, the parents will model antisocial values and behaviors. They probably did *not* reinforce stealing (that would take some stretch of the imagination); but they do not generally believe that stealing merits punishment. Therefore, the bulk of such activities would go unsanctioned. This tentative formulation is based on the simple notion that parents reinforce and punish in a manner isomorphic with their own established hierarchy of social behavior and values. That is, they *support* what *they themselves actually do.*

TABLE 4.2   Likelihood Parents Punish (from Patterson, forthcoming a)

Parent	Dependent Variable	Samples			
		Abused Child (N=19)	Social Aggressor (N=44)	Normal (N=36)	Stealer (N=54)
Father	Total aversive behavior	.328 (13)	.312 (24)	.179 (25)	.109 (41)
	Hostile	.360	.262	.195	.068
	Social aggression	.429	.408	.110	.053
Mother	Total aversive behavior	.300 (19)	.251 (44)	.189 (36)	.231 (54)
	Hostile	.259	.239	.167	.178
	Social aggression	.657	.400	.185	.056

Parents As Punishing Agents

The hypothesis is that, given an observed, deviant behavior, the parents of the Stealers are less likely to punish than are parents of Social Aggressors or Normal children. The idea was actually generated by the data, but it also fits the considerations noted above. Parents of the Stealers are themselves like adolescent delinquents. Even if not officially delinquent themselves, they have a great tolerance for its presence. On either count, parents of antisocial children should be less likely to punish aversive behavior. The data in Table 4.2 address this issue and are based on an analysis of six-second units in the interactions of parents and the identified problem child. Three different, dependent variables were examined, but all were based on observation data. Total aversive behavior was composed of the sum of 14 code categories sampling aversive behavior. Hostile and Social Aggression were based on subsets of code categories, but all were drawn from the more general list of 14 aversive categories. These subsets were based on functional analyses that had demonstrated that class members shared networks of controlling antecedents and shared consequences as well. Data were analyzed from four different samples: abused children, socially aggressive children, normal children, and stealers. The numbers in parentheses refer to the number of families involved. Typically, each estimate was based on a minimum of six to ten observation sessions in the home.

The traditional child development literature consistently reports that parents of antisocial children punish their children more than do parents of normal children. Given that stealing, socially aggressive, and abused children perform punishable behavior more often than normals, the same rate of punishment would produce higher absolute frequencies of punishment. But it is the likelihood of punishment that is the issue. Are parents of problem children more likely to punish a given offense than are parents of normal children? As shown in Table 2, both mothers and fathers of abused and socially aggressive children showed higher likelihoods of punishment than did mothers and fathers of normal children. This is true in every comparison, whether one uses the total aversive behavior as dependent variable (defined by 14 types of aversive behavior) or the subset Hostile, or the subset Social Aggression. Incidentally, there do not seem to be any overwhelming differences between mothers and fathers in this regard in any of the samples.

The finding that stands out most clearly was that *fathers of Stealers* were the least likely to punish aversive child behavior. This trend stood up regardless of the dependent variable considered. The same tendency was present for mothers only when the dependent variable was Social Aggression.

When parents punished antisocial children, there was a significant increase in the likelihood that the child would *extend* the course of deviant behavior (Patterson, 1979). In fact, for these children, parental punishment made things worse! The data in Table 4.3 address this issue in greater detail, and relate it to Stealers. The findings were analyzed separately for mothers and fathers and each of the four samples. The likelihood describes the probability that, given one child's coercive behavior was punished by a parent, a second coercive child behavior would immediately follow. The row figures labelled "corrected base rate" in Table 4.3 define the likelihood that a second coercive behavior would immediately follow the first. (The correction for the base rate values was based on those events remaining after the punished events were removed from the sample).

There seem to be very few differences between normal and socially aggressive children in their base rates, or in the likelihood of stopping when given parental punishment. The most dramatic differences appear

TABLE 4.3 Likelihood Parental Punishment Effective in Suppressing Coercive Child Behavior (from Patterson, forthcoming a)

Samples	Total Deviant Cluster				Hostile Cluster				Social Aggressive Cluster			
	(N)	Father	(N)	Mother	(N)	Father	(N)	Mother	(N)	Father	(N)	Mother
Normals	(19)	.517	(29)	.657	(18)	.541	(27)	.605	(13)	.209	(20)	.290
Corrected base rate		.76		.74		.67		.74		.35		.45
Stealers	(41)	.250	(54)	.460	(41)	.159	(54)	.441	(41)	.073	(53)	.088
Corrected base rate		.63		.79		.50		.68		.073		.17
Social aggressive	(24)	.546	(44)	.630	(21)	.334	(43)	.632	(16)	.556	(36)	.540
Corrected base rate		.69		.65		.68		.65		.35		.53
Child abuse	(13)	.730	(18)	.472	(12)	.710	(17)	.792	(13)	.821		
Corrected base rate		.73		.76		.80		.78		.74		

when one considers what happens to boys who steal. Whether one compares the effect of punishment with the corrected base rate value, or with the comparable values for normal children, it is apparent that parental punishment has little impact on children who steal. It is hypothesized that the reason for this was the inadequate pairings of parental threats with backup punishments (Patterson, forthcoming a). These parents yell, scold, threaten, and occasionally physically assault the child. The normal parent, it is believed, is more likely to back up the threats and scoldings with the withdrawal or privileges or with work details.

In effect, parents of young to-be-delinquent children (Stealers) tend to punish less, and when they do punish, it is less effective.

Some Further Considerations

The studies by Reid and Hendriks (1973) and Patterson (1979) show that if one considers the coerciveness of observable deviant behavior, the child who steals will occupy an intermediate position between normal and socially aggressive children. That is, there are a number of children who are high-rate stealers who are also socially abrasive in their interactions with other family members. But the bulk of children referred because of stealing are not observably different from Normals in their level of coercive interaction. The overwhelming impression about the homes of these children is that of a distant, uninvolved pattern of familial interaction. This clinical impression is buttressed by the findings from the Reid and Hendriks (1973) study reproduced in Table 4.4. The data from these small samples showed that Stealers were less positive and friendly in their familial interactions than either Normals or Social Aggressors. The same patterns characterize the interactions of the parents as well. Mothers of Stealers were observed to be the least friendly in their interactions with other family members.

One final bit of data is relevant to these considerations. If parenting is indeed a determining variable in delinquent behavior, then training in parenting skills should be accompanied by reductions in such delinquent acts. In an earlier study, 28 families of stealers completed a parental training program (Reid et al., 1980). During daily telephone calls, parents were asked if they had reports of their child stealing in the previous 24 hours. Twenty-eight of these families completed at least five weeks of treatment. Prior to treatment, the mean rate of stealing was .83 events per week. At termination, the average weekly rate was .07. All 28 subjects had at least one stealing event prior to treatment; five of the 28 subjects had at least one posttreatment stealing event.

TABLE 4.4 'Mean Rate Per Minute of Positive-Friendly Behavior
of Boys and Parents (from Reid and Hendriks, 1973)

	Normals	Stealers	Social Aggressors	F	p
Positive-Friendly boys behaviors	7.18	6.29	6.84	2.46	.10
Mothers	8.66	7.31	8.19	4.35	.05
Fathers	6.67	6.79	5.82	1.55	n.s.

These findings suggest that it is possible to teach parents a set of techniques that reduce stealing among their children. A six-month follow-up suggested that the effects persist. The community follow-up by Moore et al. (1979), however, shows that a year or more after treatment these parents and their children who steal reverted to their pretreatment modes of behavior.

SUMMARY

Several points of correspondence were noted between social control theories and a current version of social learning theory. Both agree that the proper question concerning delinquency is *not* why they do it: The real question concerns under what conditions they will continue to do what is normal for two- and three-year-old children. The assumption in coercion theory, a recent update of social learning theory, is that parents who cannot or will not employ family management skills are the prime determining variables. The eight-year-old antisocial child who steals or hits has been allowed to do so by his parents.

Parents can, and do, learn how to manage antisocial children. If the parents are not so trained, it is unlikely that the children will outgrow these patterns. In fact, the majority of high-rate Stealers studied around the age of nine to ten years old had at least one police contact by the age of fourteen. Young Stealers were definitely at risk for later delinquency; in fact, many became chronic offenders.

The findings suggested that mothers of Stealers perceived themselves as nonconforming, rebellious, and acting out; i.e., as delinquents. Presumably, fathers of Stealers are also like this. These values were thought to correlate with the fact that parents of Stealers do not interpret stealing events as "deviant." In that they are not deviant, they are not punished.

Antisocial acts that are not punished tend to persist. Parents of Stealers do not track; they do not punish; and they do not care.

NOTE

1. A detailed extension of the topics covered here appears in Patterson (forthcoming a).

REFERENCES

BANDURA, A. (1973) Aggression: A Social Learning Analysis. Englewood Cliffs, NJ: Prentice-Hall.

HARTUP, W. W. (1977) "Peer interaction and the process of socialization," in M. J. Guralneck (ed.) Early Intervention and the Integration of Handicapped and Non-Handicapped Children. Baltimore: University Park Press.

HATHAWAY, S. R. and E. MONACHESI (1953) Analyzing and Predicting Juvenile Delinquency with the MMPI. Minneapolis: University of Minnesota Press.

HIRSCHI, T. (1969) Causes of Delinquency. Berkeley: University of California Press.

MAHONEY, M. J. (1974) Cognition and Behavior Modification. Cambridge, MA: Ballinger.

MEICHENBAUM, D. H. (1977) Cognitive Behavior Modification. New York: Plenum.

MOORE, D. R., B. P. CHAMBERLAIN and L. MUKAI (1979) "Children at risk for delinquency: a follow-up comparison of aggressive children and children who steal." J. of Abnormal Child Psychology 7: 345-355.

NYE, F. I. (1958) Family Relationships and Delinquent Behavior. New York: John Wiley.

PATTERSON, G. R. (1979) "A performance theory for coercive family interactions," in R. Cairns (ed.) Social Interaction: Methods, Analysis, and Illustration. Hillsdale, NJ: Lawrence Erlbaum & Associates.

PATTERSON, G. R. (forthcoming a) Coercive Family Processes. Eugene, OR: Castalia.

——— (forthcoming b) "Mothers: the unacknowledged victims." Monographs of the Society for Research in Child Development.

——— (forthcoming c) "Siblings: fellow travelers in coercive family processes." Presented at the XI Annual Banff International Conference on Behavior Modification.

PATTERSON, G. R., J. B. REID, R. R. JONES and R. E. CONGER (1975) A Social Learning Approach to Family Intervention: Families with Aggressive Children (Vol. 1). Eugene, OR: Castalia.

REID, J. B., B. P. CHAMBERLAIN, G. R. PATTERSON and R. LORBER (1980) "The treatment of multiple-offending young adolescents using family treatment based on social learning principles." Unpublished.

REID, J. B., G. HINOJOSA and R. LORBER (1980) "Social learning approach to the outpatient treatment of children who steal." Unpublished.

REID, J. B. and A.F.C.J. HENDRIKS (1973) "Preliminary analysis of the effectiveness of direct home intervention for the treatment of predelinquent boys who steal," in L. Hamerlynck, L. Handy and E. Mash (eds.) Behavior Change. Champaign, IL: Research Press.

REID, J. B. and G. R. PATTERSON (1979) "The modification of aggression and stealing behavior of boys in the home setting," in A. Bandura and E. Ribes (eds.) Behavior Modification: Experimental Analyses of Aggression and Delinquency. Hillsdale, NJ: Lawrence Erlbaum & Associates.

Robert L. Burgess

Pennsylvania State University

5

FAMILY VIOLENCE:
Implications from Evoluntionary Biology

Child abuse refers to any nonaccidental injury sustained by a child under eighteen years of age resulting from acts of commission or omission by a parent, guardian, or caretaker. Such acts range from violent, impulsive, extreme physical assault to nonimpulsive, seemingly deliberate torture of a child to physical and psychological injury resulting from the abnegation of parental responsibility for the child's well-being. The definition of child abuse in the abstract is much easier to accomplish, however, than its documentation in particular instances. One reason for this difficulty in the determination of child abuse is that it is rarely observed by anyone other than immediate family members. Child abuse typically occurs behind closed doors. Most often the child's injuries are the only indicators of abuse. And since the child is often persuaded that he or she has received just and correct punishment or that drawing attention to the injury would only result in further abuse, it is only in cases of severe or repeated injury that a determination of child abuse can be made. Consequently, it would be especially advantageous to be able to predict situations which are particularly likely to result in abuse. Understandably, an increasing number of behavioral and social scientists has been motivated by this concern.

A common assumption in research on violence, aggression, and severe punishment is that they are abnormal and pathological forms of behavior. Therefore, research and theory have tended to focus on the supposed psychological deficiencies or aberrations of the perpetrators of the abusive acts (e.g., Galdston, 1965; Kempe and Helfer, 1972; Steele and Pollock, 1974) or, alternatively, upon aberrant societal values and norms or inequities and strains in the social order (e.g., Gelles, 1973; Gil, 1970). Yet, when one looks beyond the press of public concern, the clamor of the news media, and the incentives of federally financed research grants, it becomes evident that violence, aggression and the severe mistreatment of children have been with us since antiquity (Dart, 1948; Bigelow, 1969;

91

Blanc, 1962). When we examine the history of mankind, whether from paleontological evidence, documentary accounts such as the Bible, or from culture-specific myths and fairy tales we see evidence of children being mistreated, abandoned, sacrificed, or eaten. Moreover, anthropologists have frequently reported the harsh treatment of children, including disfigurement and infanticide, in culture after culture (Korbin, 1977). Nor is mistreatment of the young limited to mankind. The zoological literature is filled with rather gruesome accounts of infanticide in such species as lions and langurs (Schaller, 1972; Hrdy, 1974).

EVOLUTIONARY THEORY

Given the long history of child abuse and its generality across species and cultures, we may gain added purchase on the phenomenon by seeking theoretical generalizations that derive from an historical perspective, that transcend interspecific differences, that are sufficiently general to permit parsimonious interpretations of the diverse data presently available, and yet are precise enough to generate specific predictions. In this chapter, I shall argue that modern evolutionary theory possesses these qualifications.

Certainly the most general level of analysis that could be brought to the study of family relationships would be concerned with the phylogeny of such relationships. At this level we would be chiefly concerned with how it is that homo sapiens, in an evolutionary sense, came to solve the problems of survival and reproduction by establishing close attachments to individuals related by blood. In this section, I shall sketch the outlines of modern evolutionary biology as it relates to the issue of family relationships.

To begin with, evolutionists develop their research around the assumption that all of life has from the beginning of time been subjected to a continual process of natural selection or *differential reproduction.* Alexander (1979), an evolutionary biologist, has discussed the critical role that altruistic—or nepotistic—behavior toward close relatives has played in the evolution of human social relationships. His argument pivots on the assumption that humans have evolved to be altruistic toward their offspring and other genetic relatives. But this altruism is, paradoxically, fundamentally selfish. Our altruism is not indiscriminate; rather, such behavior, by being directed principally toward our children and relatives, has had the function of increasing the probability that our own genes are represented in succeeding generations. Technically, this is the principle of *inclusive fitness.* As outlandish as this notion may appear to persons unfamiliar with evolutionary biology, there is a growing body of evidence drawn from interspecific comparisons as well as historical analyses that the probability of altruistic behavior varies proportionately with the degree of relatedness (Alexander, 1979; Barash, 1977; Wilson, 1975). Thus, there is reason to suspect that much of our behavior today, including the universal tendency to court potential mates, to establish relatively enduring bonds with each other, to produce and care for offspring, to be jealous, and to mourn the loss of loved ones, can ultimately be explained in terms of the contributions those behaviors make to our inclusive fitness, i.e., to the transmission of our genes to succeeding generations.

I should emphasize my use of the adverb "ultimately" in the preceding sentence. For, while evolutionary biologists have emphasized ultimate explanations, i.e., the phylogenetic history of behaviors and traits, there are other important levels of explanation. Indeed, Niko Tinbergen, the Nobel Laureate, has argued that there are four separate, yet complementary, levels of causal analysis (Tinbergen, 1951). The other three levels include, first, the developmental or ontogenetic history of a phenomenon, for example, how an individual grows up to behave in a particular manner. This form of causal analysis is of particular importance to developmental psychologists and other students of socialization processes concerned with the acquisition of behavior. Another level of causation is concerned with the immediate or proximal antecedents of a phenomenon, for instance, the kind of events that prompt or elicit a behavior at a particular point in time. A familiar example would be the role of goal interference or frustration in eliciting an aggressive response. The final level of causal analysis, according to Tinbergen (1951), focuses on the adaptive significance of a phenomenon, i.e., the functions it performs for the individual actor. The role of behavioral consequences has been most systematically investigated by behaviorists in their analyses of contingencies of reinforcement and punishment (in sociology, see Burgess and Bushell, 1969). The point in all this is that a complete understanding of a phenomenon, such as a class of behavior like family violence, requires that we eventually address each of these four levels of causal analysis. Since I have argued elsewhere (Burgess, 1979) that students of domestic conflict have concentrated on developmental, descriptive, and functional levels of analysis, in this chapter I shall focus attention upon features of child abuse that derive from a concern for ultimate causation.

Before doing so, however, we must consider two important concepts of evolutionary theory. The first of these is the concept of *parental investment* (Trivers, 1972; Williams, 1966). Parental investment refers to behavior displayed by a parent which increases the reproductive potential of the child toward whom the behavior is directed at the cost of similar investment by the parent toward other or future offspring. Implicit to this definition is the notion that a parent has limited resources and a finite lifespan to expend those resources in the rearing of children. Knowing this, it would be predicted that some basis for the preferential distribution of resources and energies would be established simply because random behavior would not be adaptive in an evolutionary sense once any more selective strategy was introduced.

Examples of this adaptive quality of selective parental investment abound in the ethological literature. For example, the bonding of mother to infant has been reported for most species where there is any period of relative dependency of young on parental nurture for survival (Cairns, 1979). Bonding has the effect of making a parent selective with regard to the distribution of limited resources. Moreover, there is evidence that parental nurturance is neither dispensed indiscriminately to all conspecific young (e.g., Hrdy, 1974) nor is it invariant over a parent's reproductive lifetime (Barash, 1977). If this line of reasoning is correct, if an individual parent's investment in his or her offspring varies adaptively, then we should expect that parental care of young would be limited by circumstances which predict a reduced probability of inclusive fitness payoffs, or which involve intolerable costs for the parental effort.

A prime circumstance under which parental care might adaptively be discontinued or diminished is that of doubtful parenthood. This second important concept of evolutionary theory—*parental certainty*—has been used to explain important differences in male-female gender roles ranging from mate selection to marital interaction (Alexander, 1974; Barash, 1977). In any event, parental care appears to be selective depending on whether natural circumstances are such that parents are likely to be exposed to unrelated young and thus run the risk of investing in offspring that share none of their genes (Alexander, 1974). For example, individual recognition of eggs and chicks is commonly observed in species with dispersed nest sites (Wilson, 1975). Furthermore, such parental discrimination usually develops at precisely that stage of the youngster's developing mobility when the likelihood of confusion becomes a real possibility. For example, female flying squirrels will accept alien pups (an unlikely event in normal circumstances) up to fory days postpartum—the age at which young squirrels become capable of leaving the nest. From that moment on, strange juveniles approaching a female's nest are attacked (Muul, 1970).

However, even when parents can reliably identify their own offspring, their optimal strategy, in an inclusive fitness sense, would be to refrain from parental care should the prospects of those young surviving and reproducing be poor. Such a circumstance may be brought about by an inadequate resource base or by some deficiency in the offspring (Daly and Wilson, 1979). As Barash (1975) has noted, a parent's decision to cut losses should occur as early in the reproductive process as possible.

However, once parents have already invested a sizeable amount in off-spring, they should be willing to tolerate substantial risks before abandoning their young. Thus, the concepts of differential parental investment and parental confidence each have potential relevance for specifying situations which may increase the probability of parents abusing or neglecting their offspring. Let us now turn to the evidence.

PARENTHOOD

That there should be a positive correlation between the frequency and quality of parental investment and biological parenthood is based on the assumption that there would be selection pressures against squandering parental resources on nonkin (Daly and Wilson, 1979). Moreover, it is assumed that there would be several proximal mechanisms which would encourage discriminative parental care such as the attachment bond which results from early parent-infant contact. It would follow that surrogate parents would find it more difficult to develop deep affection for their charges. Indeed, Duberman (1975) reports that only 53% of stepfathers and 25% of stepmothers admitted having "parental feelings" toward their stepchildren. Such data suggest that the risk of abuse would be greater for stepchildren than for natural children.

In support of such a prediction, Daly and Wilson (1979) report data from four samples of physical abuse cases drawn from England, New Zealand, and the United States. In each case, only about one-half of the abused children lived in homes with both natural parents present. Although no satisfactory data on the living arrangements of children in the population at large are available, indirect information suggests that considerably more than one-half of all children live in two natural-parent households in the above three countries. Acording to the U.S. Bureau of the Census (1977a), 80% of all children lived with two parents in 1976. Glick (1976) estimated that 10% of those families included stepparents, while Daly and Wilson (1979) estimated that approximately 15% of such families had a stepparent in the home. If we can assume these figures are correct, then clearly stepchildren are especially at risk for potential abuse.

A similar pattern is found in the series of studies of abusive, neglectful, and normal families reported by Burgess and his colleagues (1978). In over one-half of the abusive families they studied there were stepchildren in the home. In 11 of those 16 cases (67%) the stepparent was the official perpetrator of the abuse. Significantly, in those families where a stepparent was also a natural parent (9 of the 11 families) the abuse was of a stepchild rather than a natural child in all but one case. Again we see that there is reason to suspect that stepparent households may be more at risk for potential child abuse.

PARENTAL RESOURCES

In addition to parenthood influencing the likelihood of an adult investing in young, I suggested earlier than an inadequate resource base may similarly decrease the probability of parental investment and thus increase the risk of abuse of a child by a parent or caretaker. We shall examine such a possibility by looking at the relationship between child abuse and SES, family size, and single parenthood.

There are strong reasons to suspect that child abuse, especially physical abuse, is correlated with social class. Gil's national survey (1970) indicated that child abuse is more likely in lower-class homes. He reported that over 48% of the abusive families had an annual income under $5,000, while the percentage of all families at this level was only around 25. Moreover, less than 1% of the abusive mothers were college graduates and only 17% had graduated from high school. Similarly, Gelles and Straus (1978) reported that parents earning less than $6,000 annually admitted abusing their children at a rate 62% higher than other parents. Importantly, these latter data relate to abuse admitted by parents through anonymous questionnaires rather than cases involving the legal system. Similarly, insufficient income has been cited as a factor in almost 50% of child abuse and neglect cases in statistics compiled by the American Humane Association (1978). In the same document, it was reported that the median family income for child abuse cases was $6,886 and for neglect cases $4,249. By way of contrast, the median income for all families with children in the population at large was $15,388 (U.S. Bureau of the Census, 1978b).

A second way to examine parental resources is in terms of family size. Holding resources constant, increasing the membership of a family should result in fewer resources available per family member, thus increasing the likelihood of conflicts of interest over those resources. Gil (1970) and Young (1964) have reported data indicating that the proportion of abusing families with four or more children is twice that found in the general population. Light's (1973) data indicate a similar pattern in England and New Zealand.

Burgess et al. (1978) in their observational study comparing abusive, neglectful, and normal families reported data which indicated that those patterns of family interaction found in abusive and neglectful families are especially likely the more children there are in the home. For example, they found that there was a strong inverse correlation between family size and the frequency of verbal and physical contact between a parent and any one child in the home. This was true for all forms of contact combined and for positive contacts such as physical affection and verbal praise. On the other hand, they found that the frequency of negative forms of parent-child interaction such as fights and verbal punishment remained stable across families of varying size. Thus, given that the other forms of parent-child contact diminished, the emotional climate in the larger families was clearly of a more negative nature. Such a pattern would probably be especially likely in low-income families where resources are already relatively scarce. In any case, accumulating evidence indicates that coercive styles of family interaction and resultant child abuse and neglect are more likely the larger the family and the greater the concomitant drain on family resources.

Our third way of examining parental resources is in terms of single versus two-parent households. Current estimates are that approximately 50% of all first marriages end in divorce. It is also true that divorce hits women hardest since over 70% of them must work and close to 85% must also care for children (Campbell, 1975), and they must do so without moral, economic, or psychological support from a husband or partner. Given the added stress produced by such a situation, we should not be surprised that single parent households are heavily implicated in cases of abuse (Friedman, 1976; Gil, 1970; Johnson, 1974) and neglect (Daly and Wilson, 1979). These findings are supported in a report by Kimball et al. (1980), where it was found that mothers in single parent families displayed rates of negative contacts with their children over twice that found in two-parent families. They also reported that in two-parent abusive, neglectful, and normal families combined there was a 26% higher rate of positive than negative interaction whereas in single parent families there was a 45% higher rate of *negative* than positive interaction. These data thus suggest that those patterns of family interaction found to be typical of two parent abusive and neglectful families are especially likely given the permanent absence of one parent. Kimball et al. (1980) qualify their data by noting that this pattern may be limited to low SES families such as those they studied. But it should also be noted that, in 1978, nearly one-half of all poor families were headed by women and more than two-thirds of poor black families were headed by women (U.S. Bureau of the Census, 1979). In sum, an inadequate parental resource base may substantially decrease the probability of parental investment whether the lack of resources is measured by income, education, the presence of many children in the home, or by single parenthood.

CHARACTERISTICS OF THE CHILD

Earlier in this chapter I argued that parental solicitude of young would be limited by circumstances associated with a reduced probability of inclusive fitness payoffs for the parent or with exceptionally high costs for parental effort. With regard to the former, we have already seen that abuse and neglect are, indeed, associated with such characteristics of a child as his or her step relationship to an abusive adult. A number of studies indicate that other child characteristics are implicated in abuse and neglect and that these characteristics usually involve either low reproductive potential for those children later in life, e.g., retardation and Down's Syndrome (Martin et al., 1974; Sandgrund et al., 1974), or they require effortful and costly care. For instance, Johnson and Morse (1968) reported that 70% of their child abuse cases showed some form of developmental problem ranging from poor speech to physical deformities and handicaps. Moreover, even the child welfare workers who dealt with these children found them hard to handle, fussy, demanding, stubborn, negativistic and unsmiling. As I have noted elsewhere (Burgess, 1979), "the child who represents an unwanted pregnancy, or who resembles a disliked or unfaithful spouse, the chronically sick child, the hyperactive child or the otherwise difficult-to-handle child may incite abusive behavior" (p. 160).

While positive parental feelings toward a child may be inhibited by overt signs of child abnormality, it is important to note that these characteristics of the child may sometimes be the consequence as well as the antecedent of parental responses to the child. In addition, these deficient parental responses may be due to factors which interfered with the mother-infant attachment process such as perinatal separation of the infant from its mother for medical reasons as in prematurity. Indeed, it is quite possible that the major factor determining whether a parent develops strong parental affection for a handicapped child is the child's early and prolonged separation from the mother at or soon after birth (Daly and Wilson, 1979). Certainly, there is strong evidence that premature children stand at risk for abuse and neglect (Klaus and Kennell, 1976; Martin et al., 1974; Hunter et al., 1978). Moreover, O'Connor et al., (1977) have experimentally demonstrated that the risk of parental mistreatment can be reduced substantially by simply providing a few extra hours of contact in the first two days after birth. In any event, again we have evidence consistent with an evolutionary interpretation of parent-child relationships.

CONCLUSION

The thesis of this chapter has been that we can better understand the long history of child abuse and its generality across species as well as cultures by seeking theoretical generalizations that transcend interspecific differences and are yet precise enough to account for the diverse data now available. I have tried to demonstrate that modern evolutionary theory has these characteristics. Taking the concept of inclusive fitness, I have described evidence to support the prediction that a parent's investment in young children would vary inversely with doubtful or stepparenthood, scarce parental resources, and unusually high costs for parental effort. Our next step should be to explore the interface between these relationships and the various proximal mechanisms which are undoubtedly implicated in the development of abusive patterns of family interaction as well as their immediate antecedents.

REFERENCES

ALEXANDER, R. D. (1979) in R. L. Burgess and T. L. Huston (eds.) Social Exchange in Developing Relationships. New York: Academic Press.
——— (1974) "The evolution of social behavior." American Review of Ecology 5 (September): 325-383.
American Humane Asociation (1978) National Analysis of Official Child Neglect. Englewood, CO.
BARASH, D. P. (1977) Sociobiology and Behavior. New York: Elsevier.
——— (1975) "Evolutionary aspects of parental behavior: the distraction behavior of the alpine accentor, *Prunella Collaris.*" Wilson Bulletin 87, 367-373.
BIGELOW, R. (1969) The Dawn Warriors. Boston: Little, Brown.
BLANC, A. C. (1962) Some Evidence for the Ideologies of Early Man. London: Methuen.
BURGESS, R. L. (1979) "Child abuse: a social interactional analysis," in B. B. Lakey and A. E. Kazdin (eds.) Advances in Clinical Child Psychology. New York: Plenum.
——— (1978) "Project interact: a study of patterns of interaction in abusive, neglectful and control families." Final Report to the National Center on Child Abuse and Neglect.
——— and D. BUSHELL (1969) Behavioral Sociology. New York: Columbia Univ. Press.
BURGESS, J. M., W. H. KIMBALL, and R. L. BURGESS (1978) "Family size and family violence." Presented at biannual meeting of the Southeastern Conference on Human Development, Atlanta.
CAIRNS, R. B. (1979) Social Development: The Origins and Plasticity of Inter-changes. San Francisco: W. H. Freeman.
CAMPBELL, A. (1975) "The American way of mating." Psychology Today (May): 37-43.
DALY, M. and M. I. WILSON (forthcoming) "Abuse and neglect of children in evolutionary perspective," in R. D. Alexander and D. W. Tinkle (eds.) Natural Selection and Social Behavior.
DART, R. A. (1948) "The Makapansgat proto-himan *Australopithecus promethus.*" American Journal of Physical Anthropology 6: 259-281.

DUBERMAN, L. (1975) The Reconstituted Family: A Study of Remarried Couples and Their Children. Chicago: Nelson-Hall.

FRIEDMAN, R. (1976) "Child abuse: a review of the psychosocial research," in Hefner et al. (eds.) Four Perspectives on the Status of Child Abuse and Neglect.

GALDSTON, R. (1965) "Observations of children who have been physically abused and their parents." American Journal of Psychiatry 122: 40-443.

GELLES, R. J. (1973) "Child abuse as psychopathology: a sociological critique and reformulation." American Journal of Orthpsychiatry 43: 611-621.

GIL, D. G. (1970) Violence Against Children: Physical Abuse in the United States. Cambridge, MA: Harvard Univ. Press.

GLICK, P. C. (1976) "Living arrangements of children and young adults." Journal of Comparative Family Studies 7, 321-333.

HRDY, S. B. (1974) "Male-male competition and infanticide among the langurs (*Presbytis entellus*) of Abu Rajasthan." Folia Primatologica 22: 19-58.

HUNTER, R. S., N. KILSTROM, E. N. KRAYBILL, and F. LODA (1978) "Antecedents of child abuse and neglect in premature infants: a prospective study in a newborn intensive care unit." Pediatrics 61: 629-635.

JOHNSON, C. F. (1974) Child Abuse in the Southeast: Analysis of 1172 Reported Cases. Athens, GA: Regional Institute of Social Welfare Research.

JOHNSON, B. and H. A. MORSE (1968) "Injured children and their parents." Children 15: 147-152.

KEMPE, C. H. and R. E. HELFER (1972) Helping the Battered Child and His Family. Philadelphia: Lippincott.

KIMBALL, W. H., R. B. STEWART, R. D. CONGER and R. L. BURGESS (1980) "A comparison of family interaction in single versus two parent abusive, neglectful and normal families," in T. Field, S. Goldberg, D. Stern, and A. Sostek (eds.) Interactions of High Risk Infants and Children. New York: Academic Press.

KLAUS, M. H. and J. H. KENNELL (1976) Maternal-Infant Bonding. St. Louis: C. V. Mosby.

KORBIN, J. (1977) "Anthropoligical contributions to the study of child abuse." Child Abuse and Neglect: The International Journal 1: 7-24.

LIGHT, R. J. (1973) "Abused and neglected children in America: a study of alternative policies." Harvard Educational Review 43: 556-598.

MARTIN, H. P., P. BEEZLEY, E. F. CONWAY, and C. H. KEMPE (1974) "The development of abused children. Part I. A review of the literature. Part II. Physical, neurologic, and intellectual outcome." Advanced Pediatrics 21: 25-73.

MUUL, I. (1970) "Intra- and inter-familial behaviour of *Glaucomys volans* (Rodentia) following parturition." Animal Behavior 18: 20-24.

O'CONNOR, S. M., P. M. VIETZE, J. B. HOPKINS, and ALTEMEIR (1977) "Post-partum extended maternal-infant contact: subsequent mothering and child health." Pediatric Research 11: 380.

SANDGRUND, A. R., R. GAINES, and A. GREEN (1974) "Child abuse and mental retardation: a problem of cause and effect." American Journal of Mental Deficiencies 79: 327-330.

SCHALLER, G. B. (1972) The Serengeti Lion: A Study of Predator-Prey Relations. Chicago: Univ. of Chicago Press.

STEELE, B. F. and C. B. POLLOCK (1974) "A psychiatric study of parents who abuse infants and small children," in R. E. Helfer and C. H. Kembe (eds.) The Battered Child. Chicago: Univ. of Chicago Press.

TINBERGEN, N. (1951) The Study of Instinct. London: Oxford Univ. Press.

(ed.) Sexual Selection and the Descent of Man 1871-1971. Chicago: Aldine.
U.S. Bureau of the Census (1979) 20 Facts on Women Workers.
—— (1977) "Marital status and living arrangements: March 1976." Current Population Reports, P-20, No. 306. Washington, DC: U.S. Government Printing Office.
—— (n.d.) "Money income in 1976 of families and persons in the United States." Current Population Reports, P-60, No. 114. Washington, DC: U.S. Government Printing Office.
WILLIAMS, G. C. (1966) Adaptation and Natural Selection. Princeton, NJ: Princeton Univ. Press.
WILSON, E. O. (1975) Sociobiology: The New Synthesis. Cambridge, MA: Harvard Univ. Press.
YOUNG, L. (1964) Wednesday's Children: A Study of Child Neglect and Abuse. New York: McGraw-Hill.

A. R. Mawson

Loyola University, New Orleans

6

AGGRESSION, ATTACHMENT BEHAVIOR, AND CRIMES OF VIOLENCE

For hundreds of years the same categories have been used by laymen and scientists to describe behavior, categories such as aggression, sex, feeding, and drinking. These categories, which arose for the most part from introspective analyses of motivation, are now so ingrained in the general vocabulary that the question is seldom raised of whether they are in fact useful for scientific purposes of description. The implicit task for the scientist tends to be considered that of explaining the various behaviors as conventionally classified. So it is with aggression. Thus, when one individual acts toward another in such a way as to cause injury or death, the injurious consequence of the behavior is assumed to be its central or defining characteristic, and the act is labeled "aggression," "assault," or "criminal homicide" when the perpetrator was believed to have con sciously intended to injure or kill his victim. The methodological result is that considerable effort has been made to explain the various manifestations of "aggression," yet the descriptive usefulness of the category itself is taken for granted.

For many interpersonal acts involving lethal or minor injury, however, it can be shown that aggression is either inappropriate description of the behavior or one which is impossible to validate. Here it is suggested that a large proportion of such acts are more usefully classified as *attachment behaviors*: that is, as proximity- or contact- seeking behaviors of high intensity. The injuries inflicted in the course of the behavior are accordingly viewed as a fortuitous result of the perpetrator's attempts to achieve intense physical contact with the victim. It is further suggested that many crimes of violence are the outcome of certain precipitating factors and a strong individual predisposition for attachment behavior.

AUTHOR'S NOTE: I thank Dr. John Bowlby for his critical reading of an earlier version of this chapter.

AGGRESSION AND ATTACHMENT
BEHAVIOR: SUGGESTIVE PARALLELS

The notion that attachment behavior and aggression are in some way related to each other has been the subject of many scattered reports in the literature. Freud (1922) noted that in almost all intimate relationships, feelings of love and hate are intermingled. Lorenz (1966) suggested that social bonds develop only in aggressive animal species, and Bernstein and Gordon (1974) have observed that strong bonding is particularly evident in pigtail monkeys, a species known for its aggressiveness. Many years ago, Simmel (1955) (and more recently Bard [1971] and Goldstein [1975]) suggested that the closer and more intimate an association between two people, the greater the likelihood of aggression. As for crimes of violence, not only does homicide involve familiars more than strangers (Ferracuti and Newman, 1974; Constantino et al., 1977), but spouse killings and slayings within the victim or offender's home are significantly more brutal than those committed against other categories of persons or committed outside the home (Wolfgang, 1958). Among violent crimes as a whole (homicide, assault, rape, armed robbery), the lethality or degree of violence is inversely related to the percentage of strangers involved in the offense (Lystad, 1975). It has been suggested on the basis of such evidence that the incidence of homicide is directly related to the strength of social attachments (Henry and Short, 1954; Mohr and McKnight, 1971).

These observations and generalizations so far remain unexplained; indeed, little attempt has been made to explain them, one reason being, perhaps, that the two sorts of behavior intuitively seem entirely unrelated to one another. Thus attachment objects are generally viewed as persons to whom feelings of love are displayed, whereas aggression is reserved for enemies. Also, in a cultural climate that values love above all else as the sine qua non of all enduring relationship, the idea seems abhorrent that attachment behavior could in some way be related to violence and murder. To state this assumption more prosaically, *attachment behavior and aggression tend to be viewed as discrete behavioral systems with unique identifying characteristics and separate, though possibly overlapping determinants.*

What I will try to show here is that much interpersonal "aggression," rather than constituting a discrete behavioral system, can be more usefully understood as the upper end of a spectrum of increasingly intense attachment or proximity-seeking behaviors. I will then argue that many crimes of violence can also be usefully explained within a framework of attachment behavior.

A comparison is first made of the determinants, targets, functional consequences, and topography of aggression and attachment behavior.

Next, the same analysis is applied to certain crimes of violence. Finally, the theory of attachment behavior is contrasted briefly with another major approach, the subculture of violence thesis.

COMPARISON OF AGGRESSION AND ATTACHMENT BEHAVIOR

Probably the most widely accepted definition of *aggression* is "any sequence of action, the goal response to which is the injury of the person to whom it is directed" (Dollard et al., 1939: 9). Moyer (1975: 161) similarly defines aggression as "overt behavior involving intent to inflict noxious stimulation or to behave destructively toward another organism." Both definitions emphasize the notion of a conscious intention to inflict injury, as distinct from accidental injury. *Attachment behavior,* as defined by Bowlby (1969: 198-209), refers to responses designed to maintain proximity to, or contact with, a particular individual. In this case, however, the motivation to seek contact is not necessarily a conscious one; nor is the accompanying emotional state necessarily one of love or affection. As applied to human infants, attachment behaviors of low intensity include smiling, relaxed locomotion, watching, and touching, while those of high intensity include rapid following, approach, and fierce clinging (Bowlby, 1969: 250). An *attachment* (or social bond) is defined in terms of attachment behavior that is preferentially directed to a specific individual over a period of time (cf., Rosenthal, 1973).

Determinants

The determinants of attachment behavior, and of aggressive behavior in general, are strikingly similar. Bowlby (1969: 259) lists the following as determinants of attachment behavior: fatigue, hunger, ill-health, pain, and cold; mother absent, departing, or discouraging of proximity; the occurrence of alarming events, and rebuffs by other adults and children. Aggression is also known to be associated with fatigue, hunger, pain, the experience of separation, rebuffs by a family member, and various alarming events (Johnson, 1972). With regard to sex differences, males appear to be more sensitive to the stress of separation than females (Rutter, 1970), and males are similarly more aggressive than females (Maccoby and Jacklin, 1974).

Targets

With regard to targets, both attachment behavior and aggressive responses tend to be directed at familiar individuals. There is much evidence that once a certain level of perceptual development has been reached, organisms tend to avoid unfamiliar stimuli and approach familiar stimuli (Salzen, 1978), a tendency that is particularly strong in situations of alarm or danger. As for aggression, the evidence is conflicting. If the targets of aggression tend to be familiar organisms, then intragroup aggression would be expected to be more frequent and serious than intergroup aggression. Reviewers of the animal literature, however, find exactly the opposite to be true. Thus Scott (1975: 247) claims that "intergroup conflict is more dangerous than that within groups," while Marler (1976: 243) states that "fighting becomes less frequent as animals grow more familiar with one another." On the other hand, in the case of human aggression, a considerable amount of aggression is known to occur between close relatives. Several writers have recently drawn attention to what is described as the "myth" that family life is usually loving and harmonious, whereas in actuality a vast amount of mild and serious aggression occurs in families without necessarily attracting the attention of the police (Gelles and Straus, 1979). Thus, whether or not intragroup aggression is more frequent and serious than intergroup aggression, the amount of human intragroup aggression is much greater than was documented until recently. The data to be reviewed shortly on crimes of violence also indicate that the largest category of victim-offender relationships in homicide and assault is that involving relatives, friends, and close acquaintances.

Functional Consequences

There is evidence to suggest that, at least under certain conditions, attachment behavior and aggression are reciprocally related to each other; that is, attachment behavior in individual A can elicit attachment behavior *or* aggression in individual B, while aggression in individual A can elicit either attachment behavior *or* aggression in individual B. For instance, the calls or cries of a child will elicit the approach of mother, and persistent crying sometimes provokes aggression (Baldwin and Oliver, 1975). Conversely, aggressive behavior is known to speed up the formation of attachments in many species (Hoffman, 1974), as well as causing the recipient of the behavior to become aggressive (Feshbach, 1970). Since aggression can induce aggressiveness or attachment behavior toward the aggressor, while attachment behavior can also induce attachment behavior or aggression toward the individual seeking proximity, there may well be some fundamental similarity in the kinds of behavior to which the labels of aggression and attachment behavior have been applied. It is to this issue which we now turn.

Topography

So far, it has been noted that the determinants, targets and functional consequences of aggression and attachment behavior are very similar, if not identical. Here it is further argued the label of aggression is very difficult and often impossible to apply to interpersonal behavior in practice, and that the observed responses can be more usefully described as highly intense attachment behavior.

The key distinguishing feature of aggression is that it is action undertaken with the intention of inflicting injury. However, the label cannot be applied to animals and preverbal children since their intentions are unknowable. In the case of human adults who are subsequently questioned about "aggressive" acts they have committed, some individuals are often unable to remember their intention at the relevant time; others may have had several intentions in addition to that of causing injury (and the problem here is to decide which was the main intention); and still others may genuinely recall never having had any clear or specific intention at the time of the act. Even when individuals claim to have acted aggressively, memories of such incidents are notoriously subject to rationalization and other forms of distortion, especially under the influence of a persistent and possibly biased interviewer (Briscoe, 1975). Thus, in most cases, the label of aggression, as defined in terms of injurious intent, is either inapplicable or must be inferred retrospectively from behavior (Bandura, 1973).

As Bandura and Walters (1963) have noted, the criterion of aggression often adopted implicitly in practice is behavioral *intensity*. However, the level of intensity at which a behavior is deemed to be "aggressive" is highly subjective. What this suggests is that acts to which the label of aggression is applied do not constitute a distinct behavioral system with unique identifying characteristics but instead represent a set of points placed arbitrarily on a spectrum of increasingly intense behavior of some other sort. But the question is, a spectrum of *what sort* of behavior? My suggestion is that this is a spectrum of proximity or contact-seeking behavior, and that such behaviors tend to be labeled "aggressive" when they exceed an arbitrary level of intensity. A smile or grin, for instance, can *widen* or *deepen* into a rageful grimace; whimpering or calling can *progress* to irate screaming; and relaxed locomotion or clinging can *escalate* into stamping, punching, pulling, biting, shaking, and other so-called aggressive acts. In short, this progression of acts may be more usefully described, not as a dichotomous switch in motivation from proximity-seeking to aggression, but as a single continuum of increasingly intense proximity-seeking behavior.

ATTACHMENT BEHAVIOR AND CRIMES OF VIOLENCE

The foregoing analysis suggests the hypothesis that many crimes of violence may be similarly reinterpreted within the framework of attachment behavior. Such crimes include murder, manslaughter, assault, aggravated assault, and familial forms of violence including child abuse and wife-beating. The general hypothesis proposed for consideration is that many such crimes are a largely fortuitous (i.e., unplanned) consequence of intense contact-seeking behavior, and that the individuals involved in such acts tend to have a strong predisposition for attachment behavior, as evidenced by a general tendency to show more intense and persistent proximity-seeking behavior than other individuals of comparable age, sex, or social background.

If this is the case, we would expect to find in reviewing the literature on criminal violence that the (1) determinants, (2) targets, and (3) topography of these crimes are very similar, if not identical, to those of attachment behavior, and (4) that the perpetrators have a strong predisposition for attachment behavior.

(1) Determinants

Summarizing from the previous discussion, proximity-seeking behavior is elicited under three sorts of conditions: (A) those involving perceived abandonment, rejection by, or separation from, an attachment object; (B) those in which the individual is the recipient of attachment behavior; and (C) those involving other kinds of environmental stress. Such conditions figure prominently in the literature on criminal violence. Thus, with regard to (A) *separation-rejection,* Mowat (1966) reported that almost a third of 63 male murderers had been separated from their wives prior to the crime, and Macdonald (1968) found that many husbands who had threatened to kill their wives had themselves been threatened with abandonment. The threat of separation has also been implicated in cases of matricide (O'Connell, 1963) and filicide (Meyerson, 1966), and children who seem unresponsive or very placid may be viewed as rejecting by a parent and become the victim of abuse (Steele and Pollock, 1974). (B) *Intense attachment behavior* in the form of insult, antagonism, threats or other so-called "aggressive" provocation can result in violence (e.g., Ferracuti and Newman, 1974). Nagging or ridicule can also provoke a child into murdering a parent (Malmquist, 1971). Such "victim-precipitated" crimes accounted for 26% of the 158 criminal homicides in Philadelphia between 1948 and 1952 (Wolfgang, 1958). Typically, a husband assaulted his wife and was then killed by her. Less intense forms of attachment behavior may also place individuals at risk for assault. For instance, Baldwin and Oliver (1975) noted that crying or screaming often led to child abuse (in a group of child-abusing families). This often led to greater screaming, and further abuse. (C) As for other *stress,* Macdonald (1968) found that more than 40% of 74 adult males who had threatened to kill their wives had recently lost their jobs or suffered business failure. Frazier (1974) found that 18 of 31 murderers in the United States had suffered severe and repeated humiliation, and Westermeyer (1972) reported that recent gambling losses and public humiliation precipitated homicidal attacks ("amok") in 8 of 32 Laotian males. Social stress, including unemployment and social isolation, has also been implicated in child abuse (Steele and Pollock, 1974).

(2) Targets

There is considerable evidence that homicide and assault are largely intragroup phenomena. Mulvihill et al., (1969) found that victims and offenders usually share similar characteristics; most violent crimes are intraracial, and most homicides and assaults take place between relatives, friends and acquaintances. Cross-cultural studies (e.g., Palmer, 1960) indicate that homicide victims and offenders are rarely, if ever, strangers. As in adult murders, children are most likely to kill a family member, friend, or acquaintance (Macdonald, 1961). Recent figures for the United States, however, indicate a marked increase in the proportion of felony murders— that is, murders committed in the course of some other crime—and hence, presumably, the killing of strangers (Rushforth et al., 1977).

(3) Topography

Crimes of violence are defined on the basis of premeditated or intentional injury, but these criteria are rarely applicable in practice. Less than 5% of all known homicides are both premeditated and intentional (Wolfgang and Ferracuti, 1967); the vast majority are unplanned and result from sudden acts of passion in which intentions are either confused, conflicting, or absent (Briscoe, 1975). If an individual actually intended to kill, we might expect him to show little or no grief following the crime. Although such is reportedly the case in some instances (e.g., Reinhardt, 1970), intense mourning and regret are more commonly encountered, certainly in child murderers (Bender, 1959; O'Connell, 1963); and among murderers as a whole, from 4% to greater than 40% subsequently kill themselves (Ferracuti and Newman, 1974); West, 1966), suggesting that feelings of grief and remorse are common. The alternative concept proposed here, that the behavior in many cases represents intense contact-seeking, would appear to be consistent with the following observations. First, attacks on other persons often far exceed the degree of intensity and persistence necessary to cause injury or death. Cases involving multiple fractures, multiple knife wounds, and severe mutilation to the point of gross dismemberment are not uncommon (e.g., West, 1966: 67). Second, many homicides and assaults are committed before, during, or shortly after sexual intercourse (Morris and Blom-Cooper, 1964). Third, it is possible to interpret attacks using knives, guns and various "blunt instruments" as providing a high degree of penetrating contact with the victim, otherwise obtainable only with the teeth.

(4) Predisposition for Attachment Behavior

Since not all individuals react with attachment behavior of such intensity to cause injury or death, it seems necessary to postulate some form of individual predisposition for seeking contact. There is, in fact, considerable indirect support for the view that murderers and assaultists have a strong predisposition for attachment behavior. This is shown by observations indicating that the bond between victim and offender is often of exceptional intensity; furthermore, there is a tendency for offenders to be extremely dependent, jealous, and/or aggressive. Recall that just as attachment behavior and aggression are believed to form a single continuum of proximity-seeking behavior, so the *traits* of "dependency" and "aggressiveness" are similarly reinterpreted as forming a single continuum, the latter being a more intense expression of the former.

Intense bonding between the parties involved in criminal violence, often to the point of symbiotic attachment, has been observed in adult murderers (West, 1966; Wolfgang and Ferracuti, 1967), in parents who murdered their children (Forrest, 1974), sons who murdered their mothers (Wertham, 1941; Sendi and Blomgren, 1975), between mother and son in cases where the son killed his father (Corder et al., 1976), in child abusers (Steele and Pollock, 1974; Smith and Hanson, 1975), and even between the parents of child abusers (Steele and Pollock, 1974). A further aspect of intense attachment is, of course, jealousy, which is frequently mentioned as a characteristic of murderers (Mowat, 1966; West, 1966) and men who have repeatedly assaulted their wives (Gayford, 1979). Such individuals also tend to be described as highly dependent and/or aggressive (West, 1966; Macdonald, 1968; Forrest, 1974), and in the case of child abusers this sometimes takes the form of a "role reversal" between parent and child (Steele and Pollock, 1974; Justice and Justice, 1976).

THE INTERACTIONAL DYNAMICS OF CRIMINAL VIOLENCE

It remains now to offer a tentative explanation of *how* the combination of precipitating and predispositional factors leads to criminal violence. The basis question is, under what conditions is attachment behavior likely to be intensified to the point of causing injury or death?

Consider a hypothetical relationship between two individuals, P and Q, one or both of whom have a strong predisposition for attachment behavior. Three basic types of conditions are suggested which, either singly or, more likely, in combination, could lead to violence. These conditions correspond to the three general determinants of attachment behavior. They are, for individual P,

(i)   attachment behavior toward P on the part of individual Q. The arrows on the diagrams indicate the initial direction of proximity-seeking. Thus, here P ◄——— Q.

(ii) separation-rejection of P by Q. Thus P   Q ——►.

(iii) environmental stress, leading P to seek contact with Q. Thus P ——► Q.

Each process is now described in turn.

(i) Attachment behavior is normally self-terminating once the preferred object has been reached (Bowlby, 1969). In the present case, P would tend to respond to Q's proximity-seeking behavior in such a way as to calm Q. If, however, as in this hypothetical situation, P overreacts to Q's efforts to make contact (e.g., by shouting instead of by offering soothing words), P's behavior provides an eliciting stimulus for increasingly intense attachment behavior on the part of Q. Thus, a positive-feedback spiraling of attachment behavior between P and Q may be set in motion, with possibly fatal results. In this situation, the process is analogous to magnetic forces (Bischof, 1975), in which attraction increases with proximity.

(ii) Here, individual Q for some reason rejects or withdraws from P—or P so interprets the behavior—and the more Q attempts to withdraw from P, the greater become P's efforts to regain proximity, again with a possibly fatal outcome. This situation constitutes a negative-feedback process, with properties somewhat analogous to those of an elastic band: The force created by the action is proportional to the degree of expansion or distance (Bischof, 1975).

(iii) A third possible condition leading to violence between P and Q is one in which P seeks contact with Q in response to stresses external to the relationship, such as unemployment or social isolation.

It should be noted that an individual with a strong predisposition for attachment behavior may not only be at greater risk of committing violence but also of being the *victim* of violence, since his behavior provides a stimulus for others to react to with reciprocally intense attachment behavior. This may help to explain victim-precipitated homicides and assaults as described, for example, by Wolfgang (1958). Where both parties in a relationship have a strong predisposition for attachment behavior the risk of violence will be increased accordingly, and chance factors may determine which of the two will take the role of victim or offender in the event of a slaying. According to theories of assortative mating, persons with such characteristics tend to seek each other out (Dominion, 1972). In this situation it is the wife who is most likely to be the victim of abuse, as suggested by Gayford's (1979) study of wife-beating. If an infant or child happens to be one of the predisposed individuals, then he or she will almost invariably be the victim. This may account for the observation that irritable babies and difficult children are particularly at risk of becoming the victims of parental abuse (Steele and Pollock, 1974; Justice and Justice, 1976). Whereas mild or even vigorous crying will elicit care and solicitousness of appropriate intensity in a normal mother (Bowlby, 1969, 1973), it would seem that the combination of a child with a tendency to cry intensely and persistently (indicating a strong predisposition for attachment behavior), and a mother whose attachment behavior is habitually persistent and intense, is a potentially very lethal one indeed.

THE SUBCULTURE OF VIOLENCE THESIS

According to the subculture of violence thesis (Wolfgang and Ferracuti, 1967), the overrepresentation of young, black, lower-class males in the statistics on violent crime results from the adherence of such individuals to subcultural values prescribing and condoning violence in response to aggressive provocation. There is, however, no clear-cut evidence as yet that individuals convicted of violent crimes tend markedly to condone or approve of violence (Ball-Rokeach, 1973; Curtis, 1978), or that approval of violence is greater among the population groups with the highest incidence of violent crimes (Erlanger, 1974). In fact, cultural values strongly opposed to violence have been reported in one exceptionally aggressive South American tribe (Bolton, 1973). The alternative thesis proposed here to account for the epidemiological facts is that what males, the young, blacks, and the lower classes have in common (in contrast to females, the old, whites, and the upper classes), is a *relatively strong predisposition for attachment behavior.* Thus, young males seem to be more sensitive to the stress of separation from an attachment figure than young females (Rutter, 1970). Second, 15 to 25 is not only the peak age for crimes of violence, but it may also be the age group in which attachment behavior is at its highest frequency and intensity in the life cycle, as evidenced by dating, marriage, and membership in social movements and organizations. Third, regarding class differences, there is evidence to indicate that the lower class is typically characterized as having tightly knit kinship networks, close ties of familiarity between neighbors, and a strong sense of communal solidarity (Goldthorpe et al., 1969). Finally, in regard to blacks, despite traditional views of black family life as "disorganized" (Moynihan, 1965), it remains a possibility that blacks in general enjoy stronger "social bonds" in the form of extended family and neighborly relations than do whites (cf., Ball et al., 1976), a supposition which could well have a bearing on the comparatively low rate of suicide among blacks, given the well-known association between isolation and suicide (Roberts, 1973). Since recent studies have shown, contrary to the usual view, that young blacks have more positive self-images than whites (Taylor, 1976), the time may have come to reconsider traditional notions about black family life as well (cf., Allen, 1978).

CONCLUSION

With the exception of the subculture of violence thesis, there have been few attempts in the professional literature to relate the empirical facts on violent crime to a theoretical framework. Theories of aggression in general have tended to focus either on the extremes of narrow, stimulus-response relationships (e.g., the frustration-aggression hypothesis) or on broad cultural determinants (e.g., the subculture of violence thesis), while neglecting the immediate social context and especially the social relationship between victim and offender. Starting with the observation that many victim-offender relationships in criminal violence involve intimates or familiars, the thesis of the present paper has been that much so-called aggressive, homicidal and assaultive behavior is an intense expression of the tendency to seek the proximity of familiar persons under conditions of stress, even when the individual toward whom the behavior is directed is the source of stress. On this view, the injuries suffered by the victim in the course of the behavior are the unplanned and unintended consequences of the perpetrator's attempts to make strong contact, albeit penetrating and sometimes lethal contact. It was further suggested that the stronger the offending individual's predisposition for attachment behavior, the greater the probability that injury will be inflicted fortuitously in the course of seeking contact.

The theory would not appear to be applicable, however, to cases where the act is premeditated and carried out in a cold and deliberate fashion, and with the specific purpose of avoiding detection, as occurs in many neonaticides (the murder of infants under twenty-four hours of age; Resnick, 1970) and felony murders. The theory does, nevertheless, provide a tentative explanation for the observations linking social bonds and violence cited earlier in the paper, and may also prove helpful in broadening current views of the violence-prone individual.

To end on a philosophical note, it is recalled that attachment behavior tends to elicit reciprocal attachment behavior in the individual toward whom it is directed, thereby strengthening social bonds. In view of this underlying, pérhaps evolutionary-adaptive purpose of attachment behavior, it is a tragic irony that the perpetrator of homicide should, by his own hand, deprive himself of the very thing we have suggested he is really seeking, and of which he appears to have a special need: namely, close physical contact with another live human being.

REFERENCES

ALLEN, W. R. (1978) "The search for applicable theories of black family life." Journal of Marriage and the Family 40: 117-129.
BALDWIN, J. A. and J. E. OLIVER (1975) "Epidemiological and family characteristics of severely-abused children." British Journal of Preventive and Social Medicine 29: 205-221.
BALL, R. E., G. J. WARHEIT, J. S. VANDIVER, and C. HOLZER (1976) "Extended kin ties: a comparison of low-income blacks and whites." Presented at the Annual Meeting of the American Sociological Association, New York City, September.
BALL-ROKEACH, S. J. (1973) "Values and violence: a test of the subculture of violence thesis." American Sociological Review 38: 736-749.
BANDURA, A. (1973) Aggression: A Social Learning Analysis. Englewood Cliffs, NJ: Prentice-Hall.
——— and R. H. WALTERS (1963) Social Learning and Personality Development. New York: Holt, Rinehart & Winston.
BARD, M. (1971) "The study and modification of intra-familial violence," in J. L. Singer (ed.) The Control of Aggression. New York: Academic Press.
BENDER, L. (1959) "Children and adolescents who have killed." American Journal of Psychiatry 116: 510-513.
BERNSTEIN, I. S. and T. B. GORDON (1974) "The function of aggression in primate societies." American Scientist 62: 304-311.
BISCHOF, N. (1975) "A systems approach toward the functional connections of attachment and fear." Child Development 48: 801-817.
BOLTON, R. (1973) "Aggression and hypoglycemia among the Quolla: a study in psychological anthropology." Ethnology 12: 227-257.
BOWLBY, J. (1973) Attachment and Loss, Vol. 2: Separation: Anxiety and Anger. London: Hogarth Press.
——— (1969) Attachment and Loss, Vol. 1: Attachment. London: Hogarth Press.
BRISCOE, O. V. (1975) "Intention at the moment of crime . . . beyond reasonable doubt." Medicine, Science and the Law 15: 42-46.
CONSTANTINO, J. P., L. H. KULLER, J. A. PERPER, and R. H. CYPRESS (1977) "An epidemiologic study of homicides in Allegheny County, Pennsylvania." American Journal of Epidemiology 106: 314-324.
CORDER, B. F., B. C. BALL, T. M. HAIZLIP, R. ROLLINS, and R. BEAUMONT (1976) "Adolescent parricide: a comparison with other adolescent murder." American Journal of Psychiatry 133: 957-961.
CURTIS, L. A. (1978) "Violence, personality, deterrence, and culture." Journal of Research in Crime and Delinquency 15: 166-171.

DOMINION, J. (1972) "Marital pathology: a review." Postgraduate Medical Journal 48: 717-725.

ERLANGER, H. S. (1974) "The empirical status of the subculture of violence thesis." Social Problems 22: 280-292.

FERRACUTI, F. and G. NEWMAN (1974) "Assaultive offenses," in D. Glaser (ed.) Handbook of Criminology. Chicago: Rand McNally.

FESHBACH, S. (1970) "Aggression," in P. H. Mussen (ed.) Carmichael's Manual of Child Psychology. New York: John Wiley.

FORREST, T. (1974) "The family dynamics of maternal violence." Journal of the American Academy of Psychoanalysis 2: 215-230.

FRAZIER, S. H. (1974) "Murder—single and multiple." Research in Nervous and Mental Disorders 52: 304-312.

FREUD, S. (1922) Group Psychology and the Analysis of the Ego. London: Hogarth Press.

GAYFORD, J. J. (1979) "The aetiology of repeated serious physical assaults by husbands on wives (wife battering)." Medicine, Science, and the Law 19: 19-24.

GELLES, R. J. and M. A. STRAUS (1979) "Violence in the American Family." Journal of Social Issues 35: 15-39.

GOLDTHORPE, J. H., D. LOCKWOOD, F. BECHOVER, and J. PLATT (1969) The Affluent Worker in the Class Structure. Cambridge, MA: Cambridge Univ. Press.

GOLDSTEIN, J. H. (1975) Aggression and Crimes of Violence. New York: Oxford Univ. Press.

HENRY, A. F. and J. F. SHORT (1954) Suicide and Homicide. New York: Free Press.

HOFFMAN, H. S. (1974) "Fear-mediated processes in the context of imprinting," in M. Lewis and L. A. Rosenblum (eds.) The Origins of Fear. New York: John Wiley.

JOHNSON, R. N. (1972) Aggression in Man and Animals. Philadelphia: W. B. Saunders.

JUSTICE, B. and R. JUSTICE (1976) The Abusing Family. New York: Human Sciences Press.

LORENZ, K. (1966) On Aggression. New York: Harcourt, Brace, Jovanovich.

LYSTAD, M. H. (1975) "Violence at home: a review of the literature." American Journal of Orthopsychiatry 45: 328-345.

MACCOBY, E. E. and C. N. JACKLIN (1974) The Psychology of Sex Differences. Stanford: Stanford Univ. Press.

MACDONALD, J. M. (1968) Homicidal Threats. Springfield, IL: C. C. Thomas.

——— (1961) The Murderer and His Victim. Springfield, IL: C. C. Thomas.

MALMQUIST, C. P. (1971) "Premonitory signs of homicidal aggression in juveniles." American Journal of Psychiatry 128: 461-465.

MARLER, P. (1976) "On animal aggression: the roles of strangeness and familiarity." American Psychologist 31: 239-246.

MEYERSON, A. T. (1966) "Amnesia for homicide ('pedicide'): its treatment with hypnosis." Archives of General Psychiatry 14: 509-515.

MOHR, J. W. and C. K. McKNIGHT (1971) "Violence as a function of age and relationship with special reference to matricide." Canadian Psychiatric Association Journal 16: 29-32.

MORRIS, T. P. and L. BLOM-COOPER (1964) A Calender of Murder: Criminal Homicide in England Since 1957. London: M. Joseph.

MOWAT, R. R. (1966) Morbid Jealousy and Murder. London: Tavistock.

MOYER, K. E. (1975) "A physiological model of aggression: does it have different implications?" in W. S. Field and W. H. Sweet (eds.) Neural Bases of Violence and Aggression. St. Louis: W. H. Green.

MOYNIHAN, D. P. (1965) The Negro Family: The Case for National Action. Washington, DC: U.S. Department of Labor.

MULVIHILL, D., M. TUMIN, and L. CURTIS (1969) "The interpersonal relationship between victims and offenders," in Crimes of Violence: A Staff Report to the National Commission in the Causes and Prevention of Violence, Vol. 2. Washington, DC: U.S. Government Printing Office.

O'CONNELL, B. A. (1963) "Matricide." Lancet 1: 1083-1084.

PALMER, S. (1960) The Psychology of Murder. New York: Crowell.

REINHARDT, J. M. (1970) Nothing Left But . . . Murder. Lincoln, NE: Johnsen.

RESNICK, P. J. (1970) "Murder of the newborn: a psychiatric review of neonaticides." American Journal of Psychiatry 126: 1414-1420.

ROBERTS, A. R. (1973) "Suicide and suicide prevention." Public Health Reviews 2: 3-30.

ROSENTHAL, M. K. (1973) "Attachment and mother-infant interaction: some research impasse and a suggested change in orientation." Journal of Child Psychology 14: 201-207.

RUSHFORTH, N. B., A. B. FORD, C. HIRSCH, N. M. RUSHFORTH, and L. ADELSON (1977) "Violent death in a metropolitan county: changing patterns in homicide, 1958-1974." New England Journal of Medicine 297: 531-538.

RUTTER, M. (1970) "Sex differences in children's responses to family stress," in E. J. Antony and C. M. Koupernick (eds.) The Child in His Family. New York: John Wiley.

SALZEN, E. A. (1978) "Social attachment and a sense of security—a review." Social Science Information 17: 555-627.

SCOTT, J. P. (1975) "Violence and the disaggregated society." Aggressive Behavior 1: 235-260.

SENDI, I. B. and P. G. BLOMGREN (1975) "A comparative study of predictive criteria in the predisposition of homicidal adolescents." American Journal of Psychiatry 132: 432ff.

SIMMEL, G. (1955) Conflict and the Web of Group Affiliations. New York: Free Press.

SMITH, S. M. and R. HANSON (1975) "Interpersonal relationships and child-rearing practices in 214 parents of battered children." British Journal of Psychiatry 127: 513-525.

STEELE, B. F. and C. B. POLLOCK (1974) "A psychiatric study of parents who abuse infants and small children," in R. E. Helfer and C. H. Kempe (eds.) The Battered Child. Chicago: Univ. of Chicago Press.

TAYLOR, R. L. (1976) "Psychosocial development among black children and youth: a reexamination." American Journal of Orthopsychiatry 46: 4-19.

WEST, D. J. (1966) Murder Followed by Suicide. Cambridge, MA: Harvard Univ. Press.

WERTHAM, F. (1941) Dark Legend: A Study in Murder. New York: Duell, Sloan & Pearce.

WESTERMEYER, J. (1972) "A comparison of amok and other homicide." American Journal of Psychiatry 129: 703-709.

WOLFGANG, M. E. (1958) Patterns in Criminal Homicide. Philadelphia: Univ. of Pennsylvania Press.

WOLFGANG, M. E. and F. FERRACUTI (1967) The Subculture of Violence. London: Tavistock.

Curtis J. Braukmann
Kathryn A. Kirigin
Montrose M. Wolf
University of Kansas, Lawrence

7

GROUP HOME TREATMENT RESEARCH:
Social Learning and Social Control Perspectives

In this article we describe the general characteristics of our social learning view of delinquency and compare it with social control theory. In the context of a specific delinquency treatment approach, we present three studies relevant to social learning and social control models. For the most part, we find that the results are consistent with both models and that the models appear to complement each other.

Our social learning conceptualization emphasizes the natural science perspective of behavior analysis (Bijou and Baer, 1978). The behavior of an individual is viewed as learned, maintained, and otherwise influenced through ongoing, reciprocal interactions between behavioral and environmental events. The interactions are reciprocal and interdependent, because environment affects behavior and behavior affects environment. Such behavior-environment interactions occur in the context of a developing individual with a unique history of such interactions and a unique physical and physiological endowment that is at a particular level of maturity. Successive, changing interactions between an individual's environment and behavior are seen as resulting in, for example, the learning of language, the conditioning of emotional and anxiety reactions to some stimuli and not to others, and the learning of norms and ranges of social behavior that are accepted, encouraged, or prohibited (Keller and Schoenfeld, 1950). Much of this learning and socialization occurs through social interactions at first

AUTHORS' NOTE: The preparation of this article and the research described were supported by grants MH15200 and MH20030 from the National Institute of Mental Health (Center for Studies of Crime and Delinquency) to the Bureau of Child Research and Department of Human Development at the University of Kansas. The authors acknowledge the helpful comments of Jay Solnick, Robert Kalle, Edward Morris, Stephen Fawcett, and Eileen Allen on an earlier version of this paper. Reprints may be obtained by writing the authors at the Achievement Place Research Project, 111 Haworth, University of Kansas, Lawrence, Kansas 66045.

with family members and later with peers and with other individuals in schools and in the broader community.

From this perspective, behavior that is designated by society as delinquent is like other behavior. It is seen as a function of the unique individual's abilities and cumulative learning in interaction with current environmental influences. Delinquent behavior may be directly and specifically taught and maintained, such as when peers model or provide positive consequences for deviant activity. Less directly, performance of delinquent behavior might be facilitated due to failures to learn, such as when a child fails to acquire skills essential for obtaining rewards and for avoiding negative consequences in conventional social units, such as the school, and is thereby more easily affected by competing, nonconventional influences such as deviant peers. Learning deficiencies may result from physiologically determined limitations in learning abilities as well as from limitations in environmental circumstances.

In behavioral analysis conceptualizations, the environment operates on behavior through antecedent and consequent events (stimuli). Antecedent events can evoke or cue behavior, the latter by signalling that a particular behavior, if emitted, is likely to produce particular consequences. Consequent events that strengthen the behavior they follow are termed reinforcers, those that weaken the behavior they follow are termed punishers. The antecedents and consequences that interact with behavior can be internal or external to the individual, social or nonsocial, learned or given in the nature of the individual (Bijou and Baer, 1978). The impact of specific antecedent and consequent events is qualified by concurrent setting events, which events may be personal (organismic) states (e.g., fatigue or being drugged) or social situations (e.g., home or school).

Many important antecedents and consequences for delinquent behavior are social, but there are, nonsocial antecedents (e.g., seeing a desired and unprotected object) and nonsocial consequences (e.g., obtaining a desired object as a result of theft) for delinquent behavior. Positive social consequences (social reinforcers) for delinquent behavior are perhaps most often provided by peers. Negative social consequences for conventional behavior are often mediated by parents, schools, and conventional peers. As described by Burgess and Akers (1966: 138-139) in their presentation of behavioral theory, the value of social consequences can be expected to vary with the "reinforcing value" of the individual or group mediating the consequences. The concept of reinforcing value is an abstraction that summarizes and indexes the overall efficacy (the effect on a given person's behavior) of the various functional cues and reinforcers mediated by a particular other person or class of persons (cf., Gewirtz, 1969). The greater the variety, range, and frequency of functional reinforcers that are mediated by the particular other person or classes of persons, the more generalized the reinforcement value is likely to be. Thus, for example, a given parent may have high reinforcing value for a child because the parent mediates affection, material reinforcers, help, companionship, and enjoyable activities for the child. In turn, the parent's differential attention and approval are developed and maintained as potent social consequences. The more that a parent has such effective, positive, social consequences to provide contingently on the child's behavior, the greater can be the parent's environmental influence (e.g., as a model and teacher) in the successive combinations of the behavior-environment interactions experienced by the developing child. The child also affects his or her social environments by mediating events that are potent antecedents and consequences for the parent's behavior.

When a child is in a relationship with an adult who has considerable reinforcing value for that child, to engage in disapproved behavior is to risk the diminution of valued social consequences. If an adult with strong reinforcing value shows disapproval of classes of behavior that include behavior that could be considered delinquent, then a child would be less likely to engage in such behavior than in approved behavior. This broadly stated contingency was described by Conger (1976) in his paper on the synthesis of social learning and social control models of delinquency.

Social control perspectives complement social learning perspectives (Akers, 1973; Conger, 1976). For example, the operation of differential personal and social consequences is a central feature of both control and learning models. Kornhauser (1979) describes social controls as "actual or potential rewards or punishments that accrue from conformity to or deviation from norms" (p. 641). These rewards and costs can be internal or external, direct or indirect. They vary with the strength of the individual's bonds to conventional social groups and norms, which, in turn, vary to the extent that the individual is involved in "rewarding social relationships that would be jeopardized by non-conformity" (p. 666). Hirschi's statement of control theory, which is the major, current, control theory formulation, is supported by considerable empirical evidence (Hindelang, 1973; Hirschi, 1969). The elements of the social bond in Hirschi's statement are attachment ties of affection and respect towards parents, school, and peers; commitment to, and investment in, conventional lines of action; involvement in conventional activities; and the belief in the moral validity of social norms.

It has been assumed in traditional control theories that everyone has sufficient motivation to engage in delinquent behavior. Individuals are free to engage in such behavior when lack or loss of conventional ties reduces the cost of deviance. This view may turn attention too simply to what motivates persons not to engage in delinquent conduct (Messinger and Bittner, 1979). As Kornhauser (1979) argues, there would seem to be no logical necessity for control theory to assume little variability in motivation across individuals to engage in delinquent behavior.

Social learning theories, on the other hand, assume that variability both in positive as well as negative motivators will affect the probability of delinquent behavior. For example, in a social learning view, social reinforcement from delinquent peers can function in the development and maintenance of delinquent behavior (Burgess and Akers, 1966: 144). This is consistent with considerable data on the independent effects of peer associations on delinquency, which are not explained by a control theory concerned only with deterrents to delinquent behavior. We would suggest that a social learning view could provide the principles and processes to explain variations in inducements for delinquent behavior within a social control framework. A useful synthesis of the two models, however, does not depend on the equivalence of the control theory concept of attachment and a learning theory concept of reinforcing value. For example, it does not necessarily follow that because a youth is influenced by delinquent peers, he must correspondingly be attached to them in the control theory sense.

Each of the three exploratory studies we will present relates to both social control and behavior-analytic, social learning perspectives. Before we present the studies, it would be useful to describe the contexts in which they were conducted. The studies were carried out in family style, community based group homes for delinquents. The homes followed the Teaching-Family treatment approach (Phillips et al., 1974). In Teaching-Family group homes, an average of six youths live with a married couple called "teaching-parents" who receive a year of professional pre- and in-service training (Braukmann, et al., 1975).

The treatment approach is consistent with our social learning perspective on the role of past learning and of current environmental influences on delinquent behavior. The goal is to encourage achievement and teach situation-relevant behavior patterns, norms (discriminations), and decision-making skills presumed to help youths become more successful. The four elements of the approach are: (1) teaching of functional skills and discriminations in areas of interpersonal relations, academic tasks, and self-care; (2) a focus on developing mutually rewarding relations between the teaching-parents and the adolescents; (3) initial motivation through a flexible, individualized token economy; and (4) mediation of peer consequences through constructive, self-government procedures.

Our own quasiexperimental group-comparison research in Kansas (Kirigin et al., forthcoming) as well as that conducted on a national scale by an independent evaluation group (Jones, 1978, 1979), has found Teaching-Family programs to be significantly more cost-effective and consumer-preferred than alternatives. These evaluations also revealed considerable variation across Teaching-Family programs in during- and post-program delinquency measures. The research we describe represents our preliminary efforts to relate variations in self-report delinquency measures to variations in theory-relevant measures of youth and staff social interactions within the group homes. The first two studies measured social interaction behavior that, in our view, were likely to be related negatively to delinquency. We attempt to argue that the interaction behavior measured in the two studies also would be predicted to be related inversely to delinquency from a social control perspective. The studies were collaborative efforts with two of our colleagues, Jay Solnick and Martha Bedlington.

In the first study (Solnick et al., 1979), we attempted to relate delinquent behavior to directly observed interaction measures presumed to indicate the teaching-parents' reinforcing value. It had been suggested by Staats (1964: 333) that reinforcing value would be related to verbal and motor approach (Gewirtz, 1961). This would be consistent with a behavioral analysis: The more that the social behavior of one individual functions as reinforcers for a second individual, the more the second individual is likely to engage in behavior producing the rewarding social behavior of the first. Being near and talking to an individual are likely to produce that individual's social behavior. It therefore seemed that measures of youth talking and proximity to teaching-parents would be indices of teaching-parent reinforcing value. If, indeed, these measures are related to reinforcing value, then, consistent with the presented social learning model, we would expect the measures to be correlated negatively with concurrent delinquent behavior. This is because the greater the reinforcing value of the teaching-parents, the more effectively they could model and provide positive consequences for conventional behavior and the more that would be risked by delinquent behavior. In like fashion, if measures of proximity and talking to the surrogate parents are likely to covary with attachment, then a social bonding control model would anticipate a similar negative relation between the measures and reported delinquency. In control theory, the greater the attachment to others the more that would be risked by delinquent behavior. Talking does seem a probable correlate of attachment. Hirschi (1969) included questionnaire measures of child talking to parents in his attachment scale and found that an index of intimate communication was related negatively to delinquency. A general questionnaire measure of amount of time spent talking to parents, however, was related only mildly to delinquency. Turning to the proximity measure, there is some evidence from our own research that proximity may reflect attachment. Observed proximity was related significantly ($r = .70$, $p < .05$) to mean youth ratings of attachment across 10 group homes where attachment was measured by scale items used by Hirschi (1969). In a replication sample of 6 additional homes, we found a correlation of similar magnitude. (Correlations of the talking measure with the attachment scale were also positive in both samples but were smaller.) We tentatively conclude that the behavioral measures reflect attachment to some degree. We are not, however, suggesting that parental reinforcing value and youth attachment are necessarily equivalent, only that they are likely to covary.

In the first study, teaching-parent couples and 57 boys residing in 10 group homes were the primary data sample. These youths had been officially processed through the courts for such offenses as theft, vandalism, running away from home, truancy, sexual offenses, and drug dealing.

Each home was visited once. Before dinner, a delinquency questionnaire was administered to each youth. After dinner, a two-hour observation session was conducted. All youths and teaching-parents were asked to remain in or around the house during this session and, as much as possible, to maintain a normal evening routine. They were paid for their participation.

Behavior was recorded using a time-interval sampling procedure involving a series of 10-second-observe and 20-second-record intervals. The observation procedure involved following a teaching-parent and observing any youth behavior that occurred with respect to that teaching-parent. Sessions typically included between 200 and 240 observation intervals. In each interval, two types of youth behavior were recorded: *Proximity* was scored for a youth if any part of his body came within three feet of the teaching-parent's body; *talk* was scored any time a youth said something to the targeted teaching-parent. The measures were highly reliable over repeated sessions and over independent observers.

The self-reported delinquency questionnaire was a 13-item scale adapted from Elliott and Voss (1974). The questions covered both status offenses and criminal offenses. Each question asked the youth whether he had engaged in a particular behavior since coming to the group home. Youths responded using a four-point ordinal scale. In separate analyses, the scale had a high test-retest reliability and was significantly related to official police and court records of delinquent behavior.

Because only 10 homes were sampled in the present study, a one-way analysis of variance determined if there were reliable differences in the mean self-reported delinquency scores across homes. Statistically reliable differences were found. Analysis of covariance determined if these differences might be a function of certain demographic variables that previous research by others had found to be related to delinquency (Conger, 1977; Empey, 1978; Wolfgang, 1972). Youths' age and length of stay in the group home, number of youths in the group home, and the population of the group home community were entered in the analysis of variance as covariates. The results indicated that these variables did not account for the differences in the criterion measure.

Spearman rank order correlations (Siegal, 1956) were computed to determine if the reliable differences in criterion measures were related to the behavioral measures. Self-reported delinquency showed high and significant inverse correlations with talk and with proximity. Significant correlations were found when status offenses and the more serious criminal offenses were considered separately. These high correlations were over home means and not over the scores of individual youths. But with subsequent, repeated observations within homes, we have found significant (but lower) correlations over individuals within homes as well.

To the extent that the behavioral measures used in the first study are indicative of reinforcing value on the one hand, and of attachment on the other, the results are consistent with both social learning and social control models. The talking and proximity measures may reflect variables other than teaching-parent reinforcing or attachment value. For example, the measures may be the degree that the teaching-parents are reinforced by being proximate to, and talking to, the adolescents. The measures also may vary with the teaching-parents' efforts to supervise and instruct the adolescents. The next study concerns measuring such supervision and instruction.

In the second study (Bedlington et al., 1979), we observed teaching-parent teaching behavior over homes. We employed a composite measure of teaching that included several types of behavior: instructions about how to do things; demonstrations of behavior; practicing; reasons which specify the natural consequences of behavior; social consequences (praise); and nonsocial consequences (token economy points). In previous applied behavioral analysis experimental research, we had found this teaching-parent behavior to be effective in teaching a variety of behaviors to group home youths (see the overview by Braukmann et al., 1975). This teaching behavior also had been found in other social learning research effectively to teach numerous types of behavior across a range of populations (Bandura, 1969). From our behavioral analytical social learning perspective, we would expect that this behavior could affect delinquent behavior because it reflects the use of known behavioral influences. We assumed that our observational samples would reflect, within broad limits, the extent that the respective couples generally provided effective instruction, supervision, and discipline, both in and out of the group home. We further assumed that the teaching-parents were using this behavior to teach and maintain youth behavior that could be classified as conventional and often as incompatible with delinquent behavior.

We think that the teaching behavior would relate to the delinquency of the youths from a social control perspective as well. The role of supervision and consequences is explicit in some versions of control theory (Austin, 1977; Hirschi, 1969; Reckless, 1967). The use of reasons which specify the natural consequences of behavior may increase the youth's "rational awareness of interests" and decrease the youth's "calculation errors," which have been recognized in control theories (Hirschi, 1969). The compatibility of the teaching measure with Hirschi's control formulation also is shown in the fact that two of the three items in Hirschi's index of intimate parent-to-child communication (presumed to measure bonding) are teaching measures under our definition: When you come across things you do not understand, do your parents help you? When they make a rule, do they explain the reason? Finally, to the extent that use of the teaching behavior encourages and produces success in conventional contexts (e.g., the group home and the school), then such use may directly and indirectly increase the youths' "achievement orientation," "ambition," and their "stakes in conventional lines of actions."[1] We think we can conclude on the basis of the above considerations that from both social learning and social control positions, teaching would be related inversely to delinquency.

In the second study, the settings were 14 community based group homes for delinquents. Each of the 14 homes was visited once for approximately two hours. The observation session began when the youths arrived home from school and continued until dinner time. The observer circulated through the house every 10 minutes observing each teaching-parent and youth for 10 seconds. Teaching-parent behavior with youths was classified as teaching or counseling or other social interactions.

Teaching was scored when a teaching-parent engaged in any one of the aforementioned sorts of teaching behavior while interacting with a youth. *Private counseling* was defined as a teaching-parent and one youth engaged in a private discussion of personal problems or treatment planning in a relatively isolated area of the house. Counseling was measured because it had been found in a national survey to be the most prevalent treatment technique employed in juvenile correction facilities (Vinter, et al., 1976). *Other social interactions* included all interactions or shared activities between teaching-parents and youths that were neither teaching nor counseling interactions. High interobserver agreement was found on each of the three measures. A fourth behavioral measure, *total interaction,* was created by combining the measures of teaching, counseling, and other social interactions. The self-reported delinquency questionnaire was adapted from Elliott and Voss (1974) and administered to the youths in a private interview format.

The analyses were similar to those employed in the previously described study. First, to determine whether the ratings of delinquency differed significantly across homes, a one-way analysis of variance was conducted. This analysis showed a significant between-home effect for self-reported delinquency. The between-home effect was further examined with correlational analyses. Spearman rank order correlations were conducted with the home as the unit of analysis to determine if the behavioral interaction measures were related to delinquency. A significant inverse relation was found between self-reported delinquency and total adult interaction with youths. But when the categories of adult interaction were considered separately, counseling and other social interactions were not significantly related to self-reported delinquency. As argued earlier, this relation is consistent with both learning and control models.

The variations found in teaching across homes were undoubtedly a function of several variables, including the quality of the discriminations made by the teaching-parents (i.e., when is what teaching called for with whom) and the extent to which the teaching-parents were reinforced for teaching. Such reinforcement for teaching would likely vary with the teaching-parents' teaching abilities, the extent to which they value influencing the youths' behavior, and the extent to which the teaching-parents are not punished effectively by the youths for attempting to influence their conduct.

Given that the two studies we have described suggest that delinquency may be strongly related to teaching on the one hand and reinforcing value or attachment on the other, we might consider possible relations between these variables. For example, some of the effect of teaching might be due to its contribution to the reinforcing or attachment value of the teaching-parent. Such a notion is consistent with earlier research (Willner et al., 1977) in which we found that the various types of teaching behavior were valued by group home youths.

Conversely, the reinforcing value of the teaching-parent might affect delinquency by enhancing teaching effectiveness. Having a high reinforcing value and a good relationship with the youths might: (1) motivate the youths to change and control their behavior in order to please the teaching-parents; (2) result in increased imitation of the teaching-parents; (3) make the reinforcers mediated by the teaching-parents more attractive to the youths; and (4) keep the youths in proximity to the teaching parents to facilitate the occurrence of teaching interactions. We speculate that there may be an interdependency between teaching and reinforcement or attachment value, a reciprocal causation where each variable amplifies the effect of the other.

The final study we will describe is an ongoing one attempting to relate delinquent behavior to delinquent peer associations. There are considerable data to indicate that associations with delinquent peers are positively related to an adolescent's delinquency (Conger, 1976, 1977; Glueck and Glueck, 1950; Hirschi, 1969; Kandel, 1973). Such associations appear to have an effect on delinquent behavior that is independent of the effects of other variables such as school performance or family attachment (Hirschi, 1969).

Delinquent association was measured by talking and proximity to group-home peers. From our perspective, we would expect a youth's talking and proximity to peers to reflect the reinforcing value of those peers for him. To the extent that the peers in this case can be assumed to be likely to prompt and reinforce delinquent behavior, a social learning analysis would expect a positive correlation between these measures of association and self-reported delinquency. With regard to a social control perspective in this study, it was noted by Hirschi (1969: 230) that independent effects of delinquent associations on delinquency are beyond the reach of traditional formulations. To date, we have collected data on 27 youths in six homes, each observed three times, and, the results are very preliminary. When scores are adjusted for home means, self-reported delinquency is significantly positively related over youths to talking to peers and nearly significantly related to proximity to peers.[2] The magnitude of the found over-youth correlations are similar (but in the opposite direction, of course) to those found within this same sample between self-reported delinquency and measures of proximity and talking to teaching-parents. Preliminary analyses suggest, however, that the peer variables and the teaching-parent variables each are related independently to delinquency. This finding is what would be expected where peer-mediated influences increase the probability of delinquent behavior. It is thus consistent with a social learning view. But it appears unexplainable by traditional control theory formulations in which peer influences are not assumed to directly encourage delinquent behavior.

The results of the first two studies were consistent with both social learning and social control postures. The data from the third study, while appearing at this point to be more consistent with our social learning analysis than with traditional control formulations, are nevertheless consistent with other data that have for the most part supported the value of such social control formulations (Hirschi, 1969). Of course, all three sets of data must be regarded as tentative. There are several obvious limitations in them, not the least of which is the inability to determine causality from correlational analyses.[3]

Our ability to show that both theoretical models are consistent with the results of the first two studies reflects a basic complementarity between the behavior analysis and social control postures. Both models focus on the relation between the individual and the environment and emphasize the importance of early socialization experiences. But the models' scope and foci differ. Social control concepts concern the relation (e.g., attachment, commitment) of the individual to society and to its social units (parents, family members, peers, and schools) and examine the effects of those relations on conventional and deviant behavior. The behavioral analysis orientation, on the other hand, is on the changing interactions between the individual's behavior and social as well as nonsocial aspects of the environment. Thus, the behavior analysis focus is at once broader— encompassing behavior other than that which might be classified as deviant or conventional—as well as more fine-grained—permitting attention to the moment-to-moment impact of preceding and consequent stimuli on social as well as nonsocial behaviors.

Behavioral analysis has been used to describe and analyze behavior across a variety of species, including such complex processes with humans as decisionmaking and problem solving. Social scientists from behavioral social learning traditions have often focused their research on observable manipulations of specific conditions and on the direct, moment-to-moment, reliable measurement of observable, specific behaviors. This approach has considerable value. It has identified some of the processes involved in: (a) the development of effective social reinforcers (Cairns, 1970; Paris and Cairns, 1972); (b) the modification of moment-to-moment behavior; and (c) the learning of complex competencies. This focus on direct measurement of specific behavior and on the relating of changes in this behavior to environmental modifications has increased the likelihood that identified behavioral influence processes would be teachable, and that thereby a behavioral technology of sorts would accumulate.

It seems to us that the social control orientation, emphasizing as it does the relation of the individual to social units (the school, the family), highlights the importance of that level of analysis for understanding and intervention. Commonly occurring social units obviously teach behavior and mediate important environmental antecedents, consequences, and setting events. The social control focus on summary characteristics of the individual's interaction with social units might neglect interaction subtleties and discrete, sequential influences, and might not emphasize the role of social learning, but it highlights the molar aspects of the behavior-environment contingency configurations involving the individual and the social environment. Taken together, the two perspectives may provide a more complete accounting of the causes of delinquent behavior than either alone.

NOTES

1. Consistent with Hirschi's (1969: 129) discussion of the relation of school success and attachment to the school, increased success in school resulting from effective teaching-parent influences (e.g., teaching) might also be seen as leading to increased attachment to school. In control theory, such attachment should relate inversely to delinquency. In this regard, the independent national evaluation of Teaching-Family programs show they are reversing preprogram downward trends in the youth's grades. These increases are continuing posttreatment. In contrast, youths' grades in the comparison homes continue down both during and posttreatment.

2. Significant, positive correlations between self-reported delinquency and talking and proximity to peers have appeared at the individual-youth level within homes (i.e., where scores are adjusted for home means). Such correlations were not found at the across-home level. Thus, it is not the mean level of peer interaction in a home that is most informative about the delinquent behavior of the participant youths. Rather, it is the amount of interaction by individual youths compared to that of their peers within their home that is related to self-reported delinquency. In other words, a youth who engages in more peer interaction than the other peers within a given home, appears, on the basis of this preliminary sample, to be more likely to report delinquent behavior than are his less interactive peers.

3. Other limitations include the fact that the samples were small and the research was limited to a specific type of treatment environment. In future research we will be able to: (1) increase our sample size; (2) measure and control for pretreatment variations in delinquency and other variables; (3) include additional criterion measures such as school performance and officially recorded delinquency; and (4) relate during-program interaction variables to postprogram delinquency and performance. More convincing demonstrations of the importance of the variables discussed in this paper might be attempted through experimental interventions.

REFERENCES

AKERS, R. L. (1973) Deviant Behavior: A Social Learning Approach. Belmont, CA: Wadsworth.
AUSTIN, R. L. (1977) "Social learning and social control: a comment." Criminology 15: 111-116.

BANDURA, A. (1977) Social Learning Theory. Englewood Cliffs, NJ: Prentice-Hall.
——— (1969) Principles of Behavior Modification. New York: Holt.
BEDLINGTON, M. M., J. V. SOLNICK, C. J. BRAUKAMNN, K. A. KIRIGIN, and
M. M. WOLF (1979) "The correlation between some parenting behaviors, delinquency and youth satisfaction in teaching-family group homes." Presented at the meeting of the American Psychological Association, New York City.
BIJOU, S. W. and D. M. BAER (1978) Behavior Analysis of Child Development. Englewood Cliffs, NJ: Prentice-Hall.
BRAUKMANN, C. J., D. L. FIXSEN, K. A. KIRIGIN, E. A. PHILLIPS, E. L. PHILLIPS, and M. M. WOLF (1975) "Achievement place: the training and certification of teaching-parents," in W. S. Wood (ed.) Issues in Evaluating Behavior Modification. Champaign, IL: Research Press.
BRAUKMANN, C. J., D. L. FIXSEN, E. L. PHILLIPS, and M. M. WOLF (1975) "Behavioral approaches to treatment in the crime and delinquency field." Criminology 13: 299-331.
BURGESS, R. L. and R. L. AKERS (1966) "A differential association-reinforcement theory of criminal behavior." Social Problems 14: 128-147.
CAIRNS, R. B. (1970) "Meaning and attention as determinants of social reinforcing effectiveness." Child Development 41: 1067-1082.
CONGER, R. D. (1977) "Rejoinder." Criminology 15: 117-125.
——— (1976) "Social control and social learning models of delinquent behavior: A synthesis." Criminology 14: 17-40.
ELLIOTT, D. S. and H. L. VOSS (1974) Delinquency and Dropout. Lexington, MA: D. C. Heath and Company.
EMPEY, L. T. (1968) American Delinquency: Its Meaning and Construction. Homewood, IL: Dorsey.
GEWIRTZ, J. L. (1969) "Mechanisms of social learning: some roles of stimulation and behavior in early human development," in D. A. Goslin (ed.) Handbook of Socialization Theory and Research. Chicago: Rand McNally.
——— (1961) "A learning analysis of the effects of normal stimulation, privation, and deprivation on the acquisition of social motivation and attachment," in B. M. Foss (ed.) Determinants of Infant Behavior. New York: John Wiley.
GLUECK, S. and T. GLUECK (1950) Unraveling Juvenile Delinquency. New York: Commonwealth Fund.
HINDELANG, M. J. (1973) "Causes of delinquency: a partial replication and extension." Social Problems 21: 471-487.
HIRSCHI, T. (1969) Causes of Delinquency. Berkeley: University of California Press.
JONES, R. R. (1979) "Therapeutic effects of the Teaching-Family group home model." Presented at the meeting of the American Psychological Association, New York City.
——— (1978) "First findings from the national evaluation of the teaching-family model." Presented at the meeting of the National Teaching-Family Association, Omaha.
KANDEL, D. (1973) "Adolescent marijuana use: role of parents and peers." Science 181: 1067-1070.
KELLER, F. S. and W. N. SCHOENFELD (1950) Principles of Psychology. New York: Appleton-Century-Crofts.
KIRIGIN, K. A., C. J. BRAUKMANN, J. ATWATER and M. M. WOLF (forthcoming) "An evaluation of the Achievement Place Teaching-Family model of group home treatment for delinquent youths." J. of Applied Behavior Analysis.

KORNHAUSER, R. R. (1979) "Underlying assumptions of basic models of delinquency theories," in S. L. Messinger and E. Bittner (eds.) Criminology Review Yearbook. Beverly Hills, CA: Sage.

MESSINGER, S. L. and E. BITTNER (1979) Criminology Review Yearbook. Beverly Hills, CA: Sage.

PARIS, S. G. and R. B. CAIRNS (1972) "An experimental and ethological analysis of social reinforcement with retarded children." Child Development 43: 717-729.

PHILLIPS, E. L., E. A. PHILLIPS, D. L. FIXSEN, and M. M. WOLF (1974) The Teaching-Family Handbook. Lawrence, KA: University of Kansas Press.

RECKLESS, W. C. (1967) The Crime Problem, Fourth Edition. New York: Appleton-Century-Crofts.

SIEGAL, S. (1956) Nonparametric Statistics. New York: McGraw-Hill.

SOLNICK, J. V., C. J. BRAUKMANN, M. M. BEDLINGTON, K. A. KIRIGIN, and M. M. WOLF (1979) "The relationship between parent-youth interaction and delinquency in group homes." Presented at the meeting of the American Psychological Association, New York City.

STAATS, A. (1964) Human Learning. New York: Holt, Rinehart & Winston.

VINTER, R. D., T. M. NEWCOMB, and R. KISH (1976) Time Out: A National Study of Juvenile Correction Programs. Ann Arbor, MI: National Assessment of Juvenile Corrections.

WILLNER, A. G., C. J. BRAUKMANN, K. A. KIRIGIN, D. L. FIXSEN, E. L. PHILLIPS, and M. M. WOLF (1977) "The training and validation of youth-preferred social behaviors with child-care personnel." J. of Applied Behavior Analysis 19: 219-230.

WOLFGANG, M. R., R. FIGLIO, and T. SELLIN (1972) Delinquency in a Birth Cohort. Chicago: University of Chicago Press.

Rand Conger

University of Georgia, Athens

8

JUVENILE DELINQUENCY:
Behavior Restraint or Behavior Facilitation?

After reviewing the findings in his recent study of several hundred high school students in Seattle, Washington, Johnson suggested that "the best theory [of delinquency] would appear to be a combination of a class-free subculture (i.e., social learning) perspective with a social bonding orientation" (1979: 140). This conclusion reflects a growing interest in the possible interface between these two approaches to understanding juvenile deviance (Akers, 1977; Conger, 1976, 1977, 1978). The purpose of this analysis is to explore further the usefulness of such a synthesis and the form it might take. To achieve this goal, we will first consider the similarities between the two positions then isolate certain critical differences between them while noting the significance of these differences for predicting empirical relations. Finally, we will suggest a framework for integrating the two approaches based on our earlier analysis and a review of relevant data.

The *social learning* perspective is a general theory of action that incorporates behavioral principles applicable to people and, often, other animal species as well. It first emerged during the 1930s as an attempt to apply lessons from research with infrahumans to the study of human development (Shaffer, 1979). In fact, there is now a wide range of viewpoints about just what such a theory might encompass, with one camp decrying the other for their "radical" or "soft" approach to the issues involved (Bandura, 1977).

Regardless of the orientation, there are certain basic tenets to the model. To begin with, the theory is aimed at understanding how people acquire certain types of behavior, maintain them in their repertoire over time and, in some cases, eventually fail to emit them as circumstances change. Behavior is thought to be acquired through trial and error learning or through the observation of models. Trial and error learning occurs when particular activities first produced valued outcomes (positive reinforcement) or avoid unpleasant events (negative reinforcement). These reponses are likely to increase in frequency under similar conditions. Conversely, if the emission of a response produces an aversive outcome, such as painful shock or the removal of a valued resource, that behavior is less likely to recur in the future, a process described as punishment. When a behavior no longer produces the consequences that maintain it, it will likely decrease in frequency or be extingushed.[1]

The processes just described represent an outline of the principles that compose operant phychology. For social learning theorists, they are the basic mechanisms maintaining or eliminating behavior (Bandura, 1977). Bandura (1977), however, has been the major proponent of the view that behavior is most likely to be acquired not by trial and error but by the observation of what others do and the outcomes their actions produce for them. That is, given the requisite physical and representational skills and a similar environment, an observer is likely to perform those sorts of behavior that reinforces a model while avoiding those that are punished. But once behavior is acquired, it will continue to occur only if reinforced at least on occasion. The most controversial issue in the field regards the role of cognition in these processes; but for our purposes, it will not be necessary to enter that debate.

In sum, social learning theorists would claim that all but the simplest reflexive behavior is acquired and maintained through observed or experienced reinforcing or punishing events.[2] No distinction is made between deviant or conforming behavior and, indeed, a ready arsenal of studies supporting the approach can be found (Akers, 1977; Bandura, 1969, 1977; Conger, 1976, 1978; McGinnies and Ferster, 1971; Staats, 1975). Importantly, much of this research has demonstrated that undesirable behavior is as likely to be produced through reinforcement contingencies as it is through prosocial activities (Endler, 1965; Solomon and Wahler, 1973).

Control theories are much more limited in scope than the social learning model (Conger, 1977). The control perspective has developed only as an explanation for deviant behavior, although it does so by examining factors that promote conformity. Specifically, control models assume that the motive to deviate is relatively constant across individuals. What varies is the strength of the bond that cements each person to the conventional social order (Hirschi, 1969; Kornhauser, 1978). Because of its several similarities with a learning approach (Conger, 1976, 1978), Hirschi's (1969) version of social control theory is the one that interests us here.

In Hirschi's (1969) formulation, juveniles are bonded to society at several different levels. They vary (1) in the degree to which they respond to the opinions and expectations of others (attachment); (2) in the payoffs they receive from, and their involvement in, conventional lines of action (commitment); and (3) in the extent to which they subscribe to the prevailing social norms (belief). The greater their attachment, their commitment, and their belief, the less free juveniles are to deviate. In effect, there is no special motive to be delinquent; rather, there are socially mediated curbs on delinquency that restrain, or if absent, fail to restrain the motivations to deviance that are common to everyone (Hirschi, 1978).

SIMILARITIES IN THE MODELS

Our discussion of social control clearly shows that the theory is one of deterrence or prevention (Hirschi, 1978). In several ways, a learning approach also locates factors that should restrain the tendency to deviate. As Austin (1977) has noted, the control theory concept of *commitment* is quite compatible with learning ideas. For example, a student who does well in school, i.e., who is adequately reinforced for conventional activities, is unlikely to risk his position by engaging in criminal behavior. The importance of commitment, especially in school, is repeatedly emphasized by both control theorists (Hirschi, 1969) and by those taking a learning approach (Burchard and Harig, 1976). Indeed, learning programs developed to reduce delinquent behavior normally include a component designed to increase involvement in academic pursuits (Burchard and Harig, 1976; Cohen and Filipczak, 1971; Phillips et al., 1973). A multitude of studies confirm the fact that academic success and other rewarding relationships in the school setting reduce the probability of delinquent behavior (Hindelang, 1973; Hirschi, 1969; Johnson, 1979).

Another area of agreement between the two approaches involves *attachment* to conventional others. To the extent that a youngster enjoys close and rewarding relationships with people, e.g., parents, who approve of conventional behavior rather than antisocial conduct, the less likely it is that the juvenile will endanger these relationships by engaging in criminal activities. Again, this theme pervades the work of control theorists (Hirschi, 1969; Kornhauser, 1978) and is also an important element in the intervention attempts of social learning practitioners (Burchard and Harig, 1976; Patterson et al., 1973; Phillips et al., 1973). Although the findings are not as consistent as those for academic involvement, most studies report that close ties to conventional others, especially parents, tend to reduce delinquent behavior (Elliott and Voss, 1974; Hindelang, 1973; Hirschi, 1969; Johnson, 1979; Linden and Hackler, 1973).

The final component in the social bond described by Hirschi (1969) involves *beliefs* that are consonant with the norms of society. A social learning view is not antithetical to the notion that such beliefs should decrease the chance of juvenile deviance, but they certainly would be considered secondary to attachment and commitment in their influence

(Conger, 1976). That is, the environmental contingencies that shape both beliefs and behavior would be of primary interest. As yet there are no data that can clarify the functional relation between beliefs and delinquency; a recent study by Johnson (1979), however, suggests that beliefs or values may be as much a result as a cause of delinquency.

In behavior restraint, then, there is little to choose between control and learning ideas. Because control theory is concerned only with delinquency, rather than being the application of more abstract principles to an area initially unrelated to the development of those principles, the control model has a clarity that recommends it. Both perspectives suggest that behavior is unlikely to occur if it risks punishment through loss of those valued outcomes associated with conventional activities for adolescents who do not experience such important ties with the conventional order, deviant activities are more likely to occur because they do not endanger these rewarding bonds. Whether one predicts from the control or learning model, then, the expected deterrent effects of formal and informal social relationships on delinquency would be about the same. But are ties to conventionality a complete explanation of delinquency?

Although he notes that some critics consider its failure to provide some additional impetus to deviate a crucial flaw, Hirschi (1969, 1978) feels that control theory is limited to the concept of behavioral restraint. In the remaining discussion, motives for delinquency will be the major issue in considering differences between the perspectives of learning and control. We will begin by suggesting that learning may account significantly for the strength of one's social attachments, and that taking such processes into account may further specify the control model. We will also consider the possibility that learning notions may provide the impetus to delinquency that control theory lacks and then determine whether or not extant data support such a model. Our primary question, then, is whether delinquency is adequately explained by identifying only those factors that restrain it. Or must we locate events which facilitate its occurrence as well?

DIFFERENCES BETWEEN THE MODELS

In comparing these models, it is worth noting that they represent entirely different *research traditions.* Psychologists representing the learning approach have examined how behavior and social relations change over time. Studies representing this perspective often manipulate the variables of interest to determine their effect on one another. Sociologists, on the other hand, tend to look at the relations between variables at one point in time, e.g., using survey questionnaires. Thus, it can be shown that a correlation exists between attachment to parents and delinquency, but the processes underlying this *outcome* are difficult to determine.

The importance of this distinction may not be clear at first glance. But it suggests relations between variables that may not be predicted by control theory alone. For example, from a social learning point of view, one would expect that parental behavior of an approving sort would reinforce a juvenile, thus strengthening the bond between parent and child. Activities by parents that demonstrate social support and approval should be: (a) negatively related to delinquency; (b) positively related to other measures of attachment; and (c) should influence the correlation between other attachment variables and delinquent conduct, since the way parents behave should largely determine the level of attachment. For Hirschi, various family attachment measures should covary, but there is no indication that one should account for the influence of another.

In an earlier study, I reported data that are consistent with social learning (Conger, 1976). The results of those analyses showed that a negative relation between certain attachment measures, i.e., communication and identification by a juvenile with his parents, will exist only if parental behavior is relatively supportive and nonpunitive. In a critique of this study, Austin (1977: 114) suggested that "conditions of reinforcement are conditions affecting the probability of attachment." That, of course, is my point. Social control theory can be more carefully specified and the relations between its indicators of bonding more adequately understood with the introduction of learning, or process, variables. This position finds some of its strongest support in Austin's analysis which demonstrated that some attachment measures may not covary postively (as they should according to control theory) when parental behavior is taken into account.

In a more recent study, Johnson (1979) also reports that attachment to parents depends on parental behavior that is reinforcing. Importantly, parental actions also affect the degree to which a juvenile is susceptible to peer influences. One important possible benefit of reinterpreting' the control perspective using social learning, then, is that processes that account for various forms of commitment, attachment, and belief may be incorporated in the model.

Although learning principles may amend control notions in beneficial ways, control theorists are by no means constrained to include explanations of bonding within their model—unless, of course, they wish to use it as a framework for intervention. A more pressing issue is whether or not control theory can adequately account for other empirical relations without modifications of some type.

Because it deals only with bonds to conventional environments, control theory does not consider factors that might vary the motive to deviate (Kornhauser, 1978). For social learning theory, the differential reinforcement or punishment, or observational learning and modeling, should operate regardless of whether behavior is legitimate or not. In fact, a major component in learning approaches to delinquency involves the ways direct or vicarious reinforcement for deviant behavior may increase the probability of delinquent acts (Akers, 1977; Burgess and Akers, 1966; Bandura, 1977; Conger, 1976, 1978; Sarason, 1976).

Substantively, the failure of control theory to predict prodelinquent group processes is a major limitation in its ability to explain available data, especially those findings that deal with the influence of delinquent peers. Hirschi (1969) acknowledges the problem in reviewing his own study of more than 1500 white, male teenagers in Northern California. For example, Table 8.1, which is a reanalysis of Hirschi's Table 52 (1969: 158), demonstrates that conventional social bonds or stakes in conformity, provide only a partial explanation of youthful misconduct.

The stakes measure in the table consists of items indicative of attachment and commitment to home and school, quite analogous to what might be called the reinforcing properties of those environments (Conger, 1976). For this analysis, the original eight category variable is dichotomized at the midpoint. The cell entries give the average number of delinquent acts by each subject, the total number of subjects in each cell, and the percentage of all subjects in the table they represent. Consistent with Hirschi's (1969) interpretation, it is clear that respondents in the high stakes category are not as likely as their less-fortunate peers to have delinquent associates. But when one or more of their friends have been picked up by the police, there is a dramatic increase in their own misconduct that rivals the effects of going from high to low stakes in the absence of delinquent peers.

Those subjects who combine few positive ties to conventionality with three or more delinquent friendships, average over six times the number of self-reported delinquencies as their exact opposites—clear evidence that we must deal with the interaction of conventional and unconventional factors to explain these data. And, although Hirschi correctly notes that group process theories must primarily deal with juveniles whose ties to society are already loosened, the figures in Table 8.1 demonstrate that the majority of respondents are in that category (64%).

Control theory admittedly cannot incorporate these group process findings; but the question remains, can social learning principles complete the model? In a previous study (Conger, 1976), I attempted to demonstrate that delinquent peers do have modeling and reinforcement influences on the deviant behavior of one another. I was able to show, for example, that delinquent friends are more likely to engage in similar than dissimilar criminal acts. Moreover, data from Hirschi's (1969) study indicated that delinquent peers spend more time than conventional youths

TABLE 8.1   Average Number of Self-Reported Delinquent Acts by Stake in Conformity and Number of Delinquent Friends

Friends Picked Up by Police	Low Stakes	High Stakes
None	.52 (258/27)[+]	.28 (229/24)
One-two	.99 (156/17)	.48 (74/8)
Three or more	1.76 (186/20)	.62 (36/4)

SOURCE: Hirschi, 1969, p. 158.
[+]Number of subjects in the cell/percentage of subjects in the table.

engaging in certain potentially reinforcing interactions, e.g., talking to each other, riding around in cars, and drinking. Social learning theory would predict that individuals are likely to engage in activities similar to those characteristics of reinforcing models. Finally, I found some evidence in the literature that delinquents tend to reinforce directly one another's rule-breaking behavior (Buehler et al., 1966).

In summarizing these findings, I suggested that delinquents may "match" their behavior to the reinforcement contingencies appropriate to a given environment. That is, even individuals with high stakes in conformity would engage in some deviant behavior in settings that would reinforce those actions. Thus, given friends who model and reward criminal activities, there should be some peer influence even for these youngsters. The matching law from operant psychology, however, also states that the time individuals spend in given settings will be proportional to the reinforcement they provide (de Villiers, 1977). Thus, juveniles well rewarded by conventional environments are less likely to spend time with delinquent associates. All of these observations are consistent with the data in Table 8.1; but the interpretation of the findings discussed thus far are post hoc and do not allow a very detailed analysis of just how learning principles might account for group effects. Fortunately, an increasing amount of data from basic research is providing the means for more adequately testing the social learning perspective. Specifically, it must be shown that adolescents are receptive to the modeling influences of their delinquent friends and that they do receive direct reinforcement from them for criminal activities.

Returning to Hirschi's study, he reports that attachment to peers is negatively related to delinquency.[3] In one table, he shows that one form of attachment ("wanting to be like one's best friends") tends to reduce delinquent involvement for those with three or more close friends who have been picked up by the police, although the same effect is not found for those subjects with one or two delinquent associates (1969: 151). For social learning theory, engaging in similar activities as friends ("wanting to be like them") is crucial if modeling influences are to be demonstrated. Reanalyzing the data in Hirschi's table revealed that fully 83% of those students with one or more delinquent friends, compared to 90% of those without such friends, want to be like them in at least a few ways. Thus, while Hirschi's contention that the friendships between delinquents are not as close as those for nondelinquents may be true, the evidence suggests that an overwhelming majority of asolescents with delinquent companions are subject to modeling influences from them. These data are consistent with those recently reported by Jessor and Jessor (1977). In a longitudinal study, they found that modeling by friends was a major contributor to deviant behavior, e.g., drug use and criminal activities.

The above findings, combined with those reported by Conger (1976) regarding the similarities of offense patterns between friends, lend support to the social learning proposal that adolescents will acquire many of their unconventional propensities by observing what their companions do. The argument for modeling influences is also bolstered by two recently reported longitudinal studies that showed that involvement with delinquent friends at one point predicts either initial or increased delinquency later on (Elliot and Voss, 1974; West and Farrington, 1977). Finally, Akers and his colleagues (1979) have reported a study of marijuana and alcohol use by adolescents that indicates that imitation of peers has a significant effect on these behaviors. Within the past two years, other research has demonstrated the effects of direct social reinforcement on delinquent activities.

In his study of approximately seven hundred high school sophomores of both sexes in Seattle, Johnson (1979) asked respondents whether their friends rewarded (approved or congratulated) illegal behavior. His intent was to determine what influence direct reinforcement would have on conduct. Factor analysis, however, showed that approval for delinquency and number of delinquent friends were not empirically discriminable. That is, to have delinquent associates is to have companions who approve of that behavior and vice versa. Indeed, peer relationships and the values they represent were the only variables that had a direct effect on self-reported delinquency. Familial interactions had an indirect influence on delinquency operating primarily through attachments to school. Attachment to school was largely determined by its reinforcing nature as measured by academic success. Again, there was no direct effect of bonds to school on delinquency; rather, its influence occurred indirectly through its negative covariation with delinquent associates and values.

In their study of over 3000 male and female, junior and senior high school students in the midwest, Akers and his colleagues (1979) obtained a correlation of .50 between marijuana use and a measure of friends' reactions to it, either approving or disapproving. Their combined measures of learning influences, which included social and nonsocial sources of reinforcement, were able to account for 68% of the variance in marijuana use. This finding is consistent with other studies that have reported strong relations between marijuana use and friends' approval (Jessor and Jessor, 1977), a result that also holds for adult samples as well (Meier and Johnson, 1978).

The finding that delinquents are likely to have lawbreaking friends is not new. It is a consistent result for most research in the area, including recent longitudinal studies where the correct temporal order of events is assured (e.g., Elliott and Voss, 1974; West and Farrington, 1977). But the mechanisms responsible for peer influence have never been well understood. The above review leads to the conclusion that social learning principles may fill this gap in our knowledge. As far as delinquent associates are concerned, the learning model is consistent with the most recent findings in the field. Moreover, there is other evidence that suggests that not only deviant friends but unconventional parents and siblings as well may positively affect the acquisition of a delinquent lifestyle (Akers et al., 1979; Jessor and Jessor, 1977; Shaffer, 1979; West and Farrington, 1977).

In sum, the data confirm that a control model must be expanded and that learning principles may be useful in accomplishing that goal. Delinquency cannot be understood by considering only factors that restrain it; we must locate those events that facilitate its occurrence as well.

CONCLUSIONS

The present discussion assessed the similarities and differences between control and learning models of delinquent behavior. Predictions from both orientations would be about the same concerning the relation between ties to conformity and delinquent behavior. There is some evidence, however, that learning principles may help to explain how the bond develops between adolescents and the conventional social order. In that sense, social learning theory may help to further specify the control 'model. On the other hand, the less abstract nature of control theory pinpoints areas of concern for the application of learning ideas in the explanation of delinquency.

Beliefs of juveniles have been somewhat ignored in this analysis, but a learning model would attempt to describe the functional relations between beliefs and delinquency, much as Burgess and Akers did in 1966. They suggested that definitions or beliefs may act as discriminative stimuli or negative reinforcers for delinquent behavior. There are no data, however, that can test the exact mechanism involved, even though it is clear that beliefs (Hirschi, 1969), definitions (Akers et al., 1979), or values (Johnson, 1979) play a role in delinquent behavior. The crucial difference between the two models concerns factors that motivate delinquency. As we have seen, peers provide an impetus for juvenile deviance, contrary to the logic of control theory. One possibility is to graft Aker's (1977) group-oriented social learning theory to the control perspective to obtain some omnibus model. I suspect that the results would be exceedingly cumbersome.

Rather, the relevant aspects of both control and differential association theories should be used for developing lower level propositions that would apply more abstract learning principles to the specific problem of delinquent conduct (Conger, 1978). At the moment it would be difficult to specify the exact form that such a model would take. I am sure, however, that the resulting theory from such a merger will be incomplete. It is becoming increasingly evident that individual differences beginning at birth, in interaction with environmental events, may influence the likelihood of engaging in criminal acts at a later time (Eysenck, 1977; Hirschi and Hindelang, 1977; Mednick and Christianson, 1977; West and Farrington, 1977). For example, differential attachment to parents probably is influenced by differences in temperament among young children (Schaefer and Bayley, 1963; Shaffer, 1979).

As West and Farrington (1977) noted in their multiyear study of youngsters in London, the factors that promote, or that fail to inhibit, delinquent behavior were clearly discernible in their first cohort of 8 year olds. As a result of their findings, they are convinced that some of the behavioral dimensions they discriminated in those youngsters who eventually became delinquent were present from birth. This finding is consistent with the notion that the same learning events may not affect moral development in the same way for all individuals (Mednick, 1977).[4] I would conclude that even a combined theory based on social learning, social control, and differential association will fall short in the explanation of our dependent variable.[5] Indeed, we may have to bring men and women back into our analyses to an extent that not even George Homans could have imagined.

NOTES

1. The minimal outline of operant principles does not fairly represent the complexity or breadth of the subject (e.g., Nevin and Reynolds, 1973). It is, however, adequate for our purposes.

2. This statement is more illustrative than entirely accurate. There are controversies in the field which it does not reflect (Terrace, 1971); although, ideally, it is the social learning position (Shaffer, 1979).

3. Hindelang (1973) found a positive relation between these two variables with rural high school students; Conger (1976) found no correlation in an urban sample.

4. The idea that individuals vary in their ability to learn social contingencies parallels control theory notions (Hirschi and Hindelang, 1977) more closely than traditional social learning principles. Although the bulk of the argument here is that social learning theory compensates for deficiencies in the control model, the reverse is also true; but it remains an issue to be addressed at a later time.

5. The present analysis has also ignored the social structural conditions that influence the social-psychological processes discussed herein. A fully developed theory, of course, must include them as well. See Akers (1977) and Kornhauser (1978) for descriptions of links between these differing levels of analysis.

REFERENCES

AKERS, R. L. (1977) Deviant Behavior: A Social Learning Approach, Second Edition. Belmont, CA: Wadsworth.

――, M. D. KROHN, L. LANZA-KADUCE, and M. RADOSEVICH (1979) "Social learning and deviant behavior: a specific test of a general theory." Amer. Soc. Rev. 44: 636-655.

AUSTIN, R. (1977) "Social learning and social control: a comment on Conger." Criminology 15: 111-116.

BANDURA, A. (1977) Social Learning Theory. Englewood Cliffs, NJ: Prentice-Hall.

―― (1969) Principles of Behavior Modification. New York: Holt, Rinehart & Winston.

BURCHARD, J. D. and D. T. HARIG (1976) "Behavior modification and juvenile delinquency," in H. Leitenberg (ed.) Handbook of Behavior Modification and Behavior Therapy. Englewood Cliffs, NJ: Prentice-Hall.

BUEHLER, R. E., G. R. PATTERSON, and J. M. FURNISS (1966) "The reinforcement of behavior in institutional settings." Behavior Research and Therapy 4: 157-167.

BURGESS, R. L. and R. L. AKERS (1966) "A differential association-reinforcement theory of criminal behavior." Social Problems 14: 128-147.

COHEN, H. L., and J. FILIPCZAK (1971) A New Learning Environment. San Francisco: Jossey-Bass, Inc.

CONGER, R. D. (1978) "From social learning to criminal behavior," in M. D. Krohn and R. L. Akers (eds.) Crime, Law, and Sanctions: Theoretical Perspectives. Beverly Hills, CA: Sage.

―― (1977) "Rejoinder." Criminology 15: 117-126.

―― (1976) "Social control and social learning models of delinquent behavior: a synthesis." Criminology 14: 17-40.

de VILLIERS, P. (1977) "Choice in concurrent schedules and a quantitative formulation of the law of effect," in W. K. Honig and J.E.R. Staddon (eds.) Handbook of Operant Behavior. Englewood Cliffs, NJ: Prentice-Hall.

ELLIOTT, D. S. and H. L. VOSS (1974) Delinquency and Dropout. Lexington, MA: D. C. Heath.

ENDLER, N. W. (1965) "The effects of verbal reinforcement on conformity and deviant behavior." J. of Social Psychology 66: 147-154.

EYSENCK, H. J. (1977) Crime and Personality. London: Routledge & Kegan Paul.

HINDELANG, M. J. (1973) "Causes of delinquency: a partial replication and extension." Social Problems 20: 471-487.

HIRSCHI, T. (1978) "Causes and prevention of juvenile delinquency," in H. M. Johnson (ed.) Social Systems and Legal Process. San Francisco: Jossey-Bass.

——— (1969) Causes of Delinquency. Berkeley: University of California Press.

——— and M. J. HINDELANG (1977) "Intelligence and delinquency: a revisionist review." Amer. Soc. Rev. 42: 571-587.

JESSOR, R. and S. L. JESSOR (1977) Problem Behavior and Psychosocial Development: A Longitudinal Study of Youth. New York: Academic Press.

JOHNSON, R. E. (1979) Juvenile Delinquency and Its Origins: An Integrated Theoretical Approach. New York: Cambridge University Press.

KORNHAUSER, R. R. (1978) Social Sources of Delinquency: An Appraisal of Analytic Models. Chicago: University of Chicago Press.

LINDEN, E. and J. C. HACKLER (1973) "Affective ties and delinquency." Pacific Soc. Rev. 16: 27-46.

McGINNIES, E. and C. B. FERSTER (1971) The Reinforcement of Social Behavior. Boston: Houghton Mifflin.

MEDNICK, S. and K. O. CHRISTIANSEN (1977) Biosocial Bases of Criminal Behavior. New York: Gardner.

MEIER, R. F. and W. T. JOHNSON (1977) "Deterrence as social control: the legal and extralegal production of conformity." Amer. Soc. Rev. 42: 292-304.

PATTERSON, G. R., J. A. COBB, and R. S. RAY (1973) "A social engineering technology for retraining the families of aggressive boys," in H. Adams and I. Unikel (eds.) Issues and Trends in Behavior Therapy. Springfield, MA: Charles C Thomas.

PHILLIPS, E. L., E. A. PHILLIPS, D. L. FIXSEN, and M. M. WOLF (1973) "Behavior shaping for delinquents." Psychology Today 7: 74-79.

SARASON, I. G. (1976) "A modeling and informational approach to delinquency," in E. Ribes-Inesta and A. Bandura (eds.) Analysis of Delinquency and Aggression. Hillsdale, NJ: Lawrence Erlbaum & Associates.

SCHAEFER, E. S. and N. BAYLEY (1963) "Maternal Behavior, child behavior, and their intercorrelations from infancy through adolescence." Monographs of the Society for Research in Child Development 28.

SHAFFER, D. R. (1979) Social and Personality Development. Monterey, CA: Brooks/Cole.

SOLOMON, R. W. and R. G. WAHLER (1973) "Peer reinforcement control of classroom problem behavior." J. of Applied Behavior Analysis 6: 49-56.

STAATS, A. (1975) Social Behaviorism. Homewood, IL: Dorsey.

TERRACE, H. S. (1973) "Classical conditioning," in J. A. Nevin and G. S. Reynolds (eds.) The Study of Behavior. Glenview, IL: Scott Foresman.

WEST, D. J. and D. P. FARRINGTON (1977) The Delinquent Way of Life. New York: Crane Russak.

ABOUT THE AUTHORS

CURTIS J. BRAUKMANN is Research Associate and Assistant Professor at the University of Kansas where he is Co-Director of the Achievement Place Research Project. He is a member of the Board of Editors of the *Journal of Applied Behavior Analysis*. His several research, review, and conceptual articles concern behavior analysis, social learning approaches to treatment, and staff training in delinquency treatment.

SIDNEY N. BROWER is Associate Professor of the School of Social Work and Community Planning at the University of Maryland at Baltimore and a planner with the Baltimore City Department of Planning. His interests include human territoriality and the links between resident use patterns and physical and symbolic elements in the landscape.

ROBERT L. BURGESS is Professor of Human Development at The Pennsylvania State University. He has published numerous articles in professional journals dealing with such topics as theory construction, criminal behavior, drug use, social cooperation, patterns of communication, social exchange and power. He is co-author (with Don Bushell, Jr.) of *Behavioral Sociology: The Experimental Analysis of Social Process*. He also has a book (with Ted L. Huston) *Social Exchange in Developing Relationships*. For the past several years, Dr. Burgess has directed a series of studies exploring the dynamics of family interaction in abusive, neglectful, and normal families. This effort has let to several publications and to presentations at national and international conferences.

RAND CONGER is Assistant Professor of Sociology at the University of Georgia. His research interest is the effect of social influences on the development of deviant and conforming behavior. This interest is reflected in his empirical work on delinquent conduct, family violence, formal and informal deterrence and social processes in face-to-face interaction.

DANIEL P. DOYLE is a graduate student in sociology at the University of Washington. With Stark he has written several papers on religion and deviance, most recently a study of suicide. He also is completing a study of ethnic intermarriage based on a recoding of the 1900 U.S. Census.

MICHAEL GOTTFREDSON teaches in the School of Ciminal Justice at the State University of New York at Albany. Formerly he was the Director of the Criminal Justice Research Center in Albany, New York. He has co-authored (with Michael Hindelang and James Garofalo) *Victims of Personal Crime: An Empirical Foundation for a Theory of Personal Victimization* (Ballinger, 1978) and is co-editor of the annual *Sourcebook of Ciminal Justice Statistics* (U.S. Government Printing Office). He has been engaged in research projects involving victimization surveys, parole decision-making, and pretrial release decision-making. His current research project is a feasibility study of bail decision guidelines. Currently he is an associate editor of the *Journal of Research in Crime and Delinquency*.

STEPHEN D. GOTTFREDSON is the Director for the Criminal Justice Studies Program at the Johns Hopkins Center for Metropolitan Planning and Research. His research interests include risk screening, offense seriousness, criminal justice system evaluation, and community crime prevention.

TRAVIS HIRSCHI is Professor of Criminal Justice at the State University of New York, Albany. He is the author/coauthor of *Delinquency Research* (1967, Free Press), *Causes of Delinquency* (1969, University of California Press), and *Measuring Delinquency* (forthcoming).

LORI KENT is a graduate student in sociology at the University of washington and has written papers on religion and deviance with Stark. Currently she is analyzing the connections between juvenile delinquency and adult crime based on a national, longitudinal sample of U.S. males.

KATHRYN A KIRIGIN is Assistant Professor of Human Development at the University of Kansas, where she is also Research Associate in the Bureau of Child Research and Co-Director of the Achievement Place Research Project. She is a member of the Board of Editors of the *Journal of Applied Behavior Analysis*. Her several publications describe procedural and program outcome research on behavioral approaches to delinquency treatment.

ANTHONY RICHARD MAWSON, an interdisciplinary sociologist, is Associate Professor in the Department of Criminal Justice, Loyola University, New Orleans. His research interests focus on crimes of violence, suicide, stress, and collective behavior. He is presently completing a monograph on "transient criminality."

RODNEY STARK is Professor of Sociology at the University of Washington. He has written seven books and scores of articles on topics ranging from deviance to religion. At present he is completing a deductive theory of religion.

RALPH B. TAYLOR is an applied psychologist at the Center for Metropolitan Planning and Research, John Hopkins University. He was affiliated with the Department of Psychology at Virginia Polytechnic Institute and State University from 1977-1979. His research interests include density, territoriality, neighborhoods, and community crime prevention.

KAREN WILKINSON is an assistant professor of Sociology at Memphis State University. Her research interests are the linkage of family related variables and juvenile delinquency and the etiology of female crime and delinquency. As a graduate student, her interest in the broken home's effect on delinquent behavior led to the publication of her "The Broken Family and Juvenile Delinquency: Scientific Explanation or Ideology?" (*Social Problems* Vol. 21, June, 1974).

MONTROSE M. WOLF is a Professor of Human Development at the University of Kansas. He received his Ph.D. from Arizona State University when that psychology department was known as "Fort Skinner in the desert." He was the first editor-in-chief of the *Journal of Applied Behavior Analysis* and has been President of the Society for the Experimental Analysis of Behavior. He has written or cowritten many articles describing behavioral research with a variety of behavioral problems of autistic, retarded, delinquent, and normal children and youth.